Being There
for Someone in Grief

Being There for Someone In Grief

ESSENTIAL LESSONS FOR SUPPORTING
SOMEONE GRIEVING FROM DEATH, LOSS, AND TRAUMA

MARIANNA CACCIATORE

raku press • Novato, CA

raku press
Novato, CA 94945
www.rakupress.com
publisher@rakupress.com

ISBN: 978-0-9844541-0-5

Edited by Rebecca Salome, rebsalome@gmail.com; and Doug Adrianson, dougadrianson@gmail.com
Cover Design by Nicole Lanzotti, nlanzotti@yahoo.com
Cover Photo by Richard Petrillo, www.richardpetrillo.com
Book Design by Michael Lommel, michael@karinalibrary.com
Typeset by Karin A. Kinsey, www.dolphinpress.com
Typeset in Gentium and Calligraphy
Printed in USA
First Edition

For Susan Brady

That her death might count for more
than the sorrow that followed in its wake.

For my parents, Ray and Jo,
whose exquisite love saved me.

For Susan's parents, Norma and Jim,
and her siblings, Mike, Tim, Tom, and Nancy.
May the legacy of Susan's life, told in the stories of healing
in the pages of this book, offer you comfort.

Table of Contents

Gratitudes

Rebecca Salome, Queen of Words—with each insight offered on behalf of a future reader, and with keen sensitivity to this writer, your literary roots and tender heart have influenced the shape of this book. And, of course, in keeping with the esteemed station of a queen, you got in the last word! Mark Nepo, Gail Orchier, Geralyn Gendreau, Sharon Bard, Barbara McHugh, and Susan Hagan—our friendship came first, collaboration followed, a superb way to work. Your way with words and your kindness, insights, and honesty have made me a better writer and a better person. Thank you. Doug Adrianson—you showed up at the right time, in the perfect way, so much so that I am convinced you were divinely sent. Wayne Muller—what I have learned from you about human nature and writing has deeply enriched my life. Thank you, my friend, for this and the many years of working together. Raymond Hanson and Kathleen Epperson—your skill and care show up on every page. Thank you. Michael Lommel—your counsel in book design and publishing has been a godsend. You are a true book lover with an impeccable eye for detail. Nicole Lanzotti, Design Diva—I knew you would do a fabulous job, and of course you did. Bravo. Richard Petrillo—thank you for always giving with no strings attached. You are a man truly generous of spirit. Karin Kinsey—much gratitude for your care and precision in bringing this book into form. Jeanne-Marie Grumet—thank you for passing the salt. It's the best spice in the rack.

Izetta Smith and Susan Whitney—you were my first teachers and my best teachers. There are thousands today who, without ever knowing you, owe a debt of gratitude for your ability to skillfully teach, with beauty and grace, all you know about healing grief. On behalf of those who have had the good fortune to work with you, thank you for entrusting us with your knowledge and wisdom. Teresiana Zurita—I am grateful for your leadership at Children to Children and your deep and lifelong friendship; your brilliant insights and impeccable honesty. I especially thank you for seeing me the way you do. It is a reflection that has helped me to flourish. Linda Hardy and Liz McCusker—my deepest gratitude for all you've done to grow Children to Children into the remarkable program it is today. Your vision, integrity, and persistence have been the essential enzymes to help it thrive as it has. Thank you. You enter my heart each day as you cross the threshold. Edward McCain, Laura Cohen, and Ginny Phillips—thank you for your courage. Your stories continue to inspire me, and now many others. May they become modern-day legends. To the families I worked with at Children to Children and whose stories grace the pages of this book, I am deeply grateful for your courage to heal. May you go with ease.

Theresa Petrillo, Anita Claney, Dee Wildermuth, Megan Schrag-Toso, Rebecca Salome, Kathleen Bertolini, Margaret Meyer, Teresiana Zurita, Mary Beth Stepanek, Christine Donohue, Jayanti Alpert, Kathy-Ann DeLucia, Gail Orchier, Sharon Bard, Betsy Rothstein, and, posthumously, Ramona

Lucero—Women of my Heart. You have *been there* for me through it all—the joy, the heartache, the failures and triumphs. You're so good at it, *you* could have written this book. I love you.

Greg McGlaze—in the most honest way and with no conditions, you have loved me from the day we met. Thank you for your eloquent support, and for making me laugh more than I ever thought possible. And lucky me, I *get* you, so I get *you* (and your fabulous kids, Aidan, Shannon and Ian).

To my remarkable family, those of origin and through marriage—we have been through so much together and you have believed in me through it all. How blessed I am. I reserve the most tender place in my heart for each of you. I love you so. The Cacciatore's—Ray, Josephine, Steve, Cathy, Melissa, John, Paul, Jerry, Amy, Marie and Joe. The Petrillo's—Theresa, Pat, Renée and Robert.

Foreword

Wayne Muller

My work with Hospice showed me that the greatest gift we ever offer anyone in our lives is something we rarely value: namely, our gentle, unhurried, receptive presence. I learned that our deepest heart's time and attention is perhaps the most eloquent description of what we call *Love.*

It is difficult to imagine wishing for anyone more lovingly attentive than Marianna Cacciatore. Marianna has literally spent the bulk of her life listening for where life refuses to wither, especially in the presence of the most painful loss, grief, and death.

I have been privileged to witness her tender, intuitive presence bring miraculous healing with children, youth and adults. She teaches us that *Everyone has within them everything they need to heal.* But she also reminds us that even when we love, we still have our own work to do. She offers priceless gifts, potent in their simplicity that can help us all bear fruitful witness to that inner strength and healing in anyone who struggles with the ache of grief and loss. In these times, the soul can feel so terribly dark and barren. Marianna presents us with an elegantly simple practice, a blessed map for anyone who has ever sought to offer comfort, nourishment, or honorable companionship to someone who feels shredded by the loss of someone precious in their lives.

This is not a feel-good book to make everything seem better. It is a piercingly beautiful, courageous pilgrimage through the darkest night of the soul. Still, in the end, we cannot help but rejoice at the healing light that refuses to be extinguished, lifted up by the alchemy of honest company and presence, relentless faith, and the gift of simple, loving attention.

You may very well find yourself offering Marianna the deepest gratitude for the gift of what she reveals, in these pages, for the healing of all.

Introduction

Susan Brady and I were inseparable—best friends from the moment we met. A few days before Christmas in 1965, Susan disappeared. Just like Susie Salmon in the novel and film *The Lovely Bones,* weeks of anguish passed before police found her dismembered body.

But my Susan was not a fictional character in a book. She was real. Her murder left me with a penetrating ache so deep that it became a pivot point in my youth, forcing me out of innocence overnight. At age eleven I trusted no one enough to reach out and ask for help. There was no one to listen to the roiling thoughts in my head or bear witness to the terror I felt. No one protected me from the nightmares that came each time I closed my eyes.

Twenty-three years after Susan's murder, my childhood experience inspired me to create Children to Children, a support center for grieving children and adults. *Being There for Someone in Grief* begins with my journey through grief, and unfolds into the lives of the many people with whom I've worked. Each story of healing is accompanied by introspective insights that offer up the essential things we must know in order to *be there* for someone in their darkest hour.

I didn't do the work alone. Many volunteers from all walks of life, of different ages and from varied cultures, showed up on Children to Children's doorstep to offer their help. They were ordinary people who felt a calling. We trained them and put them to work helping those in our community—children and adults—to heal from profound losses.

Grief and loss are inevitable. In the span of a lifetime, each of us will be called on to be there for others we love and care about as they grieve, just as one day we will need friends to be there for us. We respond to this call by doing it, by courageously facing the sorrows as well as the joys of life. *Being There for Someone in Grief* explores the sweet, mysterious terrain where we all take turns loving, grieving, and holding one another through the unavoidable pain of loss.

We opened our doors and they came, lots of them: children, teenagers, parents, grandparents. At one time or another, in intimate conversation, most who were grieving said that those who loved them—their parents, their best friends, their siblings—had no clue how to be helpful. Instead, family and friends came armed with advice. They talked too much and had no sense of how to listen generously. They were uncomfortable with tears. They tried to fix. Sometimes they made demands. Other times they disappeared altogether.

Those who were grieving had no strength right then to teach their family and friends how to be helpful; most of their precious energy was being directed toward healing from their loss and simply surviving each day.

Over the years, I've tried to find simple ways to help ordinary people know what to do and remember *how to be* when in the company of someone in sorrow. A simple acronym, SALT—as in the salt of tears—emerged as a teaching tool to help *learn by heart* four basic premises for support. Four chapters in the book, a chapter for each letter, are dedicated to illustrating each skill:

* See them.
  Allow them.
  Listen to them.
  Trust them.

If you can simply **See** those in grief without acting on the urge to do something right away, you have taken the first step toward helping them to heal. Your unconditional compassion, without criticism and without your own projection, will **Allow them to do what they need to.** They may need to talk; your best response would be to **Listen** generously, without interruption, without asking questions or telling your own story. And finally, **Trust** that within them is everything they need to traverse this difficult path. They do not need your rescue. They need your quiet, steady faith in their resilience.

If you are a person in the midst of grief, this book was written on your behalf. When friends call and ask if there is anything they can do to help, you can ask them to read this book as a gift to you, and perhaps in honor of the person who died. Invite them to take this journey with you.

If you are someone who wishes to walk beside a grieving friend in a way that is welcomed, helpful, respectful, and kind, this book was written for you—to be used as a trusted guide. Here you will learn how to be present for another in the unpredictability that death brings. It offers a general map of the landscape you will journey as you learn how to gaze into the face of suffering without running away. You will also become skilled at being present for yourself, noticing your own fears and losses while being available to another.

The stories and insights offered here will assure you we are all on a journey from birth to death and that the person you love who is grieving will return from that dark night, although both of you may be changed. This book will help you learn to stay, even when it's hard. And if you should decide to *be there* authentically and intimately for someone who is grieving, a miraculous thing can happen: *Love can heal grief's wound.*

With gratitude,
Marianna Cacciatore

from the poem

YES, WE CAN TALK

Having loved enough and lost enough,
I'm no longer searching
just opening,

no longer trying to make sense of pain
but trying to be a soft and sturdy home
in which real things can land.

These are the irritations
that rub into a pearl.

So we can talk for a while
but then we must listen,
the way rocks listen to the sea.

And we can churn at all that goes wrong
but then we must lay all distractions
down and water every living seed...

—Mark Nepo

No longer was it simple,
for within the joyful notes
were woven the somber...

—Annette Childs-Oroz
Will You Dance?

I
Into the Unknown Territory

ON A winter's day in 1965, as we trudged through the crisp snow and brittle ice, traveling the well-worn path home, Susan and I had our first real fight. I had no idea how much I would regret it.

Susan Brady and I were twin sisters of different mothers. We were inseparable, beginning the day we met—a humid August day in 1962 when she drove her shiny blue bike up my driveway. I was eight years old and had just moved from an ethnic neighborhood rich with old trees and friends I'd known since birth to a suburban one in Illinois, with manicured lawns and a cul-de-sac at the end of my street. Instead of the spacious porches I had loved with a passion at my old house, homes here had cement stoops so small that when the front door opened, a person sitting there had to move. I hated this new place—until, at the end of the long and insufferable summer, I met Susan.

With her green eyes, tousled caramel hair reflecting the summer sunlight, and freckles that seemed to dance on her cheeks, Susan rescued me and helped me adjust to my new life in suburbia.

Three years later—on the eve of the winter Solstice, the longest night of the year—I moped around for hours, still upset about our fight earlier, and was in no mood for dinner when I was asked to set the table. It was already pitch black outside and had begun to snow when my father came in from work; an icy breeze burst through the door with him.

We had just begun eating when the phone rang. I jumped up and answered it, full of a wild hope that it was Susan calling to say she missed me as much as I missed her. Instead it was Susan's mother, Norma, asking if Susan was at our house. I told her she went to Chris's house after school and I gave her Chris's phone number. My family went on with dinner but I was preoccupied, hurt that Susan was still with Chris, imagining them having so much fun that Susan didn't want to leave; imagining she would choose Chris to be her new best friend.

A few minutes later the phone rang again and this time my dad took the call. I watched him as he listened, then he put his hand over the receiver and asked me, "Marianna, do you have any idea where else Susan might have gone? She left Chris's house about an hour ago and she isn't home yet."

I put my fork down, suddenly not hungry at all. "No. I have no idea." Maybe she was just taking her time walking home. I heard him say, "I'll be right there."

Susan's mom and dad were gathering a few neighbors to help search for her, and my father was going to join them. I wanted to go, but he refused in spite of all my pleas. I was her best friend! I could find her!

"No. Stay right here," he said and closed the door behind him. I ran into our formal living room at the front of the house and drew open the curtains so I could see him back the car down the driveway and drive into the dark. Furious at him and worried about Susan, I pressed my face to the plate glass and watched the snow accumulate in the indigo night.

I started thinking again about the fight we'd had on our way home from school for lunch. During the summer, Susan and I had begun learning the new language of swear words. We'd figured out that people swore mostly when something went wrong. If we wanted to swear, we needed a reason to cuss. So we tried it out. We'd be listening to a record of the Four Seasons on the phonograph in my basement—the rec room that my father made for us with wood paneling and speckled Formica shelving. We'd scratch the record on purpose and say, "Damn it." As soon as we were comfortable with certain terms like *shit* or *damn* we stepped it up.

"Shit, it's hot as hell."

"Damn it, the chain came off my bike."

"God damn it, Susan, what are you trying to do, run me off the road?"

I knew I shouldn't be swearing, but I wanted to be cool. The only problem was, I had been taught that it was a sin. On the days that we swore I was afraid to fall asleep, obsessively thinking of my bedtime prayer: *If I should die before I wake, I pray the Lord my soul to take.* In the dark of night I would wonder, *How many people die in their sleep? Do kids die in their sleep?* I feared that I would die with a sin on my soul, then go to hell.

For months I'd been afraid to tell Susan about my nightmares. I knew she would make fun of me. Summer turned to fall, and we upgraded to the word *fuck*. Neither of us had any idea what it meant; we just knew it was worse than the words we'd been saying. I hesitatingly said it a couple of times, and on those nights my bad dreams became nightmares.

3

I was desperate. I had to tell Susan. Christmas vacation would begin the day after tomorrow, and I knew we'd be playing more, which meant we'd be swearing more. I got up my courage on our way home for lunch that day. It was freezing and the sky was gray. The red scarf and stocking cap my mother had knitted for me covered all but my eyes. Through the yarn I bravely said, "Yesterday we said F-U-C-K, and last night I didn't get to sleep till midnight. And then I had a really bad dream and woke up. After that I couldn't get back to sleep at all. It's giving me nightmares and I can't do it anymore."

"You didn't have a nightmare because you swore. You just had a nightmare," she said.

She was walking a couple of steps ahead of me, swinging her arms, so sure of herself. I sped up a little to try and even up with her. I could feel my heart beating, my face flush. "No. It's because of the swearing. It's a sin."

"Who cares? People swear all the time. Nothing happens to them."

She sounded so nonchalant. Susan didn't have the same idea I had about the ramifications of sin. The nuns at the school where I had begun my education wore black dresses that covered every part of their bodies, their faces tightly framed in starched white boxes. Skin puffed out around the rigid white cloth, and when they spoke about *sin, hellfire, purgatory,* or *limbo,* their eyes seemed to grow larger, their skin more red. For Susan, those words had no power. She shrugged them off.

"What if I *die* before I can get to confession?" I said, voice rising, divulging my secret fear. I was standing in front of her and walking backwards now, spreading my arms wide to help dramatize my distress.

"You're not going to die," she said offhandedly.

4

Now I was angry. I wanted to be heard. For three years, Susan had been the only one who was really there for me. And now she was letting me down when I needed her most!

"*I know I'm not going to die,* but it *feels* like I will," I said with an urgency that was pressing on me.

Before long we were screaming at each other. "You're just a baby!" she shrieked.

"I am not!"

"Then prove it and swear!" she screamed back.

"No!" I was furious. We were standing in front of her house by now.

"Fine," she said. "I'll just hang out with Chris after school. *She'll* swear with me."

"Fine. See if I care." I stomped away. My face felt hot. The scarf was in my hands, no longer covering my neck or face. It didn't matter. My whole body was on fire with anger as I walked home replaying the fight over and over again in my mind.

LEAVE THE LIGHTS ON

Now, as my father searched the dark streets for Susan, I stood at the living room window, staring into the night. Gradually a fantasy emerged: Susan was walking up my driveway and motioning for me to be quiet and come outside. Then she would tell me where she'd been and why she wasn't going home. I would sneak food to her and hide her until she was ready. She could hide in the small, sheltered space between the wall of our home and the hedges in front. Because of the overhang of our roof and the warmth from our house, snow did not accumulate there. It was the perfect hiding place.

But she never appeared, and I became more frightened as that longest night progressed. My father came home once and announced that she hadn't been found yet. A few minutes later he went back out into the cold, black night, illuminated only by the feathery white snow that continued to fall. It was late, I was tired, and my anger at Susan had melted by now. I thought perhaps she was hiding on purpose to scare me into swearing with her. It worked. What remained were fear, regret, and a dose of defiance. I didn't care one bit about sin and, in fact, I would have happily said *fuck* a million times in front of the Pope if I could only have her back.

When my mother finally said that I had to go to bed, I could not imagine what it would be like for Susan if she arrived while we were asleep and found we had turned out the lights. I asked if we could leave all of the lights on through the night so if Susan came to our house, she would know that we loved her.

~~~

When morning came, I raced into the kitchen, certain Susan was back and to find out where she had been. I knew I'd hear the real version from her later. Instead, my weary parents told me she was not home yet. No one knew where she was.

It isn't true. Susan knows where she is! She's hiding somewhere. Susan, where are you? It's OK to come back home now. You've made your point. Come here first, to my house. I'll protect you. I'll swear with you. I'll do anything!

Days passed. Christmas came and went. My gift for Susan sat unopened beneath the tree.

By mid-February I still could not allow myself to think that Susan was dead. I had a fantasy she would reappear as suddenly as she left and everyone would be so happy just to

6

have her back, we'd tell her it didn't matter where she'd been. She was home; that was all that mattered. And then, much later, when she and I were alone, the only person she would tell her story to was me.

Susan Brady, 11 years old, 1965

Not till we are lost, in other words, not till we have lost the world, do we begin to find ourselves, and realize where we are and the infinite extent of our relations.

—Henry David Thoreau, *Walden*

2
A Time for Denial

Between the moment when a person hears of the death of someone they love and the moment when they really feel and know the truth of it, there is *time*. The psyche trails behind the piercing truth of the loss, creating a strange perception of reality. The clock seems to slow down, or perhaps the opposite happens: Time passes and they don't know where it went. A talk they had with someone is completely forgotten. Nothing seems real or important.

Slowly, weeks and months pass. They begin the long sojourn—remembering and forgetting over and over again that the person they love is dead. This journey is more "otherworldly" when the loss is sudden and there is no warning, no time to prepare.

Everything Changed

Two months after Susan disappeared, her body was found. She had died at the hands of a 25-year-old man who lived nearby. Parts of her burned, dismembered body were found in an incinerator behind his garage. The police tracked him down by following the lead given by another little girl he had tried to pick up the same night Susan disappeared. This other girl was able to describe his car, which led the police to his home. Armed with a search warrant, they found traces of Susan's body on a workbench in his garage, her blood on a hatchet, and some of her bones in the incinerator.

He said he didn't murder her. He accidentally hit her with his car as she crossed the street. On the way to the hospital, she died and he panicked. Afraid, he took her to his home, and in his garage he dismembered her body, disposed of some parts at the place where he worked, and burned the rest.

I didn't know anyone who believed his story, but during the trial, because no one had actually seen him pick her up, he was able to establish reasonable doubt. In the end he was sentenced to 33 years in prison.

Considering Susan had been missing for almost two months, you might think I would be prepared for the news, but I had been convinced she was hiding somewhere by choice. All of my thoughts were based on the presumption that Susan was orchestrating this event. This was my shield: denial protecting me from a reality too harsh to face. I could not let myself imagine anything else.

Denial had been my friend before the news of her death, and it remained my friend in the days ahead, revealing the truth slowly over time, as though it were a soft cushion designed to guard my psyche. Susan was no longer here and I did not want this to be true. With my whole little being, I did not want this to be true. Even as arrangements were being made for her memorial service, I remained sure that Susan would walk though the door, as she had always done.

Tell Me the Story, Again

In the early stages of grief, denial is not something to be fixed. The dance of remembering and forgetting that someone we love had died has a life and rhythm of its own. It will find its balance point. If you want to be helpful, your work is to develop faith in this natural process so that you can let things unfold as they will, without interference or drama. Let it be.

With really young children, it is a "gone-ness" over time that helps them to understand the finality of the words *dead, death, and died.* The enchanting "present-moment" quality in children causes them, in one moment, to ask mama when daddy is coming home from work, and then before going to sleep that same night, ask to be told again the story of how daddy died. They may ask for the story every night for a very long time. That is how the gone-ness registers as forever gone: through the telling of the story, repeatedly, as though each recitation chips away—little by little—at the denial.

If you are the parent, this is hard, really hard—telling the story until the fabric of it has worn down to loose thread and the truth has arrived in your child's mind. It's not that children don't understand the story the first time. It's not a matter of understanding at all. In fact, they know the story so well that if the storyteller varies it, even in the slightest, children will often correct them and wait until it is retold the "right way" before letting the tale go on. It's the repeated telling that makes it true for them.

Poetry has the capacity to awaken us—to turn us away from our linear way of thinking to an inner *knowing* that is not so black and white. The poet David Whyte skillfully captures this intimate journey of denial and truth in this poem:

NEWS OF DEATH
for Tom Charlotte

Last night they came with news of death
not knowing what I would say.

I wanted to say,
"The green wind is running through the fields
making the grass lie flat."

I wanted to say,
"The apple blossom flakes like ash
covering the orchard wall."

I wanted to say,
"The fish float belly up in the slow stream,
stepping stones to the dead."

They asked if I would sleep that night,
I said I did not know.

For this loss I could not speak,
the tongue lay idle in a great darkness,
the heart was strangely open,
the moon had gone,
and it was then
when I said, "He is no longer here,"
that the night put its arm around me
and all the white stars turned bitter with grief.

Nothing like Susan's murder had ever happened in our safe Midwestern town. It was a place where people left their doors unlocked, where children played outside till dusk became too dark to see one another. The shock of Susan's murder sobered everyone. Parents kept a vigilant eye on their children. When playing outside we stuck together, and curfews were earlier. But in 1966, in my small town, grief was a private matter. Big emotions were hidden or buried. As I looked around, no one was crying. Everything seemed the same as it had always been. Fathers went to work. Children went to school. Mothers packed lunches and kept homes clean. On the inside, I felt hysterical. Because no one else looked hysterical, I thought there was something wrong with me. I had nowhere to turn. The only thing I knew to do was pretend I was fine. If I acted very good at school and at home, no one would know how really out of control I felt.

THE PRICE OF HOLDING BACK OUR TEARS

Long before I met Susan I had learned to hold back tears. I must have cried a lot as a small child—I remember hearing the worn-out adage "big girls don't cry" often. I was teased incessantly by my brothers when I cried. So, by sheer force of will, I locked down my little eight-year-old body, pressed on my emotions, and taught myself to stuff it. It seemed easier that way. I'd been doing it for years, but now I was really stuck. The tears that came as I began to accept the truth of Susan's death were harder to hold back than any tears I had ever before tried to repress. My eleven-year-old self didn't know that this time my crying would not make my parents angry, didn't know that this time my brothers wouldn't tease me. I had already married tears and shame in my mind. And no one around me showed me anything different.

13

Each person grieves in a unique way. Their response depends on age, life experience, personality, environment, and other things. Woven into the variations are three common reactions, especially from young people, when an important person in their life has died: They withdraw, act out, or overachieve.

When they withdraw, they are saying, "If I disappear, nothing like this can ever happen to me again." They become very small, compliant, and careful not to attract too much attention.

Kids who act out are like a blinking neon sign saying, "Look over here. I'm in trouble. Someone come help." Therapists say these kids are the healthiest, even though it doesn't appear that way. By acting out, they are drawing attention to the family so that help arrives. Adults can act out too by abusing substances, overspending, or betraying an intimate partner, to name a few.

Overachieving children get the least amount of intervention or support. The adults in their lives usually marvel, "She is handling this so well. Her grades haven't suffered. She's keeping up with sports and her other extracurricular activities." She's doing everything she can to not only look normal, but to look good. Adults also do this really well—their grief going underground, undetected for years, while they masterfully manage their homes and careers.

My inner trauma finally spun out one day. I was in our formal living room, the room I had retreated to when my dad joined the search for Susan, the room I was in when my mom told me Susan had been murdered. With no warning, I suddenly went into a trance, an uncontrollable episode in which the phrase *"This is only a dream. This is only a dream,"* repeated itself loudly over and over, very fast in my head. I felt as if I was going to fall to the ground or float away, my legs were going to give out or disappear. I gripped a nearby chair as though my life depended on it. Round and round it went—*"This is only a dream. This is only a dream."* No matter what I did, I could not stop it. After a minute or two, the thought stopped on its own. I "came to" and remembered the heartrending, sobering truth that it wasn't a dream. It was real: Susan was dead. Susan had been murdered. Murder could happen in the world I lived in. Children could be chopped up and burned.

After that day, it occurred a couple of times a week. Each time, it felt like I was splitting in two—one part living in the real world without Susan, the other part in a world where this murder was only a bad dream.

In bed, after the lights were out, was the hardest time for me. During the day I could keep myself busy but at night I was alone with my thoughts. No one knew about our fight. No one knew it was because of me that she was so far away from home after dark. I was afraid to tell. After her body was found and we knew how she'd been murdered, visions of cut off arms and legs plagued me. Now, in addition to preserving my secret, I had to block the images from coming into my mind, and hold back the tears. All I could do as I lay in bed was pray and plead, "Please, make it go black. Make it go black. Make it go black," until I fell asleep.

Love Without Limit

Susan had lived just a few doors away. Her home was as familiar as mine. Her mother, who looked liked Doris Day, had the warmest smile of all of my friends' mothers and blue eyes that shone and sparkled. I cherished being there when Susan's dad came home from work. He would put his arms around his wife and kiss her the way couples did in movies. Susan and I would watch and giggle. I secretly imagined that one day my husband would kiss me that way.

It was awkward for me to stay away from Susan's home. I wanted to visit her mom and dad, but I was afraid. *What would I say? What would I do?* I knew it would be hard for them to see me but I had to go. On a frigid January day a few weeks after Susan vanished, I asked my mom to go with me. I was not prepared for what we found. Norma, Susan's mother, had large dark circles under her eyes. Her face was lined where before it had been smooth. Her eyes were gray, no sign of that lively blue. Her hair was dull and unstyled; her skin, pale. She wore no beautiful, pink lipstick. This was a face filled with sorrow, even when she made the astounding effort to greet me with a smile.

They led us to their basement family room, where we sat and talked. But I couldn't wait to get out of there. My heart felt like an open wound with freezing wind blowing through it, burning the surface of the skin inside. I remember thinking: *Oh, this is how it is. When you have a child, you don't choose how much you love. You love completely. And then, if something bad happens to your child, like getting kidnapped, your pain is as big as your love. I can "make it go black," but she can't turn it off.*

When we returned home, I retreated to our basement and sat on the couch in the dark. The pain I had been feeling for weeks was so difficult to stave off that I could not imagine it being worse. But it was. Looking into Norma's eyes, I had seen it. And I was afraid of that pain.

I couldn't articulate it then, but now I see that I was struggling with the risk we take when we love. As a child I was smart enough to see what had happened to Norma's heart, but not wise enough to know it could one day heal. I could only see the catastrophe and, as a result, I created a dilemma for myself. I had loved Susan from the day I met her. My enthusiasm was unbounded. There was no thermostat on my love. I had no idea love was so risky. But now I knew. I told myself with the conviction of a martyr, "I will never again love anyone as much as I loved Susan. I will not take that risk again.

"And I will never have children."

The task is not to seek for love, but merely to seek and find the barriers within yourself that you have built against it.

—Rumi

3
The Inner Journey of Grief and Healing

May 1980

From my journal:

For the third time this week, I am startled and suddenly awake in the dark early morning hours. My heart is pounding. I hear Susan's voice saying, "Everything is going to be all right." I recognize the dream, although later in the day, the only part I remember is her voice, that one sentence: "Everything is going to be all right."

When morning comes I'll call mom to ask if she has a photo of Susan. I need to see her face again. Why am I dreaming of her every night? Is she really assuring me that everything will be all right? Will it? I'm about to walk away from my marriage to a man who loves me. We haven't even been married one year. But I don't want this baby. I'm going to have an abortion and once I do that, I can't stay. He wants children. He's still young. He'll find someone else, someone who's wanted babies all her life. I don't love him anyway. I made a mistake.

Bill was a native San Franciscan, a handsome dark-haired man I'd met when I was managing a clothing store. We liked each other right away and it grew into easy relationship and a passionate one. Having grown up in San Francisco, he had lots of friends here—guys he'd known since grade school. They reminded me of the friends I left behind when I moved here from Illinois. Our weekends were filled with activity: a barbecue on Sunday, dinner in the city on Friday night, a ball game on Saturday. Bill loved all things baseball.

When it came to values and life goals, Bill and I were compatible, with one glaring exception: I didn't want children. He believed I would change my mind in time, and I can see how he might have thought that. We spent a lot of time with two of Bill's married friends who already had kids, and I played with them. He saw our easy rapport and was so confident I'd want kids of my own one day that he actually convinced me I would change. He said my maternal clock just hadn't started ticking yet. After all, I'd grown up in a family with four kids. All of my aunts and uncles had kids. When I was younger and said I didn't want children, my father always said I'd change my mind, that children and family are what make life meaningful. I guess I wanted to believe Bill and my dad. I wanted a meaningful life.

The photo of Susan arrived today. I remember this picture. It was the one they used in all of the newspaper stories, as though this was the only photo ever taken of her. One thing surprises me. Although it's in a frame now, someone had crumpled up Susan's picture and ripped it. Was it me? I don't remember. It looks like it's been pressed back into shape and preserved, maybe for this very moment. Whoever did this, thank you. For this prescient act of kindness, I thank you.

I scheduled the abortion and began finding fault with ev-everything Bill did. I hated his little blue Volkswagen bug with 150,000 miles on it. I hated how he listened to sports on the radio every chance he got. I resented his lack of ambition.

I was finding fault with him because it would be easier to leave this way. I was far too immature, too emotionally unde-veloped to see the connection between my promise never to love anyone as much as I loved Susan and the risk of loving Bill. If I could place the blame on him, I wouldn't have to look at my own complicated past. It was a coward's way out. I used the anger and judgment to steel myself in order to go through with the abortion. I had no reservations about my right as a woman to choose not to have this child—it was keeping the truth from Bill that troubled me. My dilemma was I didn't trust myself to hold firm to my conviction if he objected. I was in this position precisely because he had convinced me I would want children one day. If he talked me into having this baby, what would I do if, after the baby was born, I still didn't want to be a mother? I couldn't take the chance. I wanted out.

I had the abortion today. Bill thinks I'm in bed with stomach cramps from PMS. He has left me alone and I am grateful for this. He wants me to get rid of the photo of Susan on the night-stand. He says it's creepy. I won't do it. She feels like a guardian watching over me.

After the abortion, staying in the house with Bill became unbearable. I couldn't keep up the charade. It reminded me of the months after Susan's murder and the unbearable secret I kept about how we'd fought on the day she died. I never told anyone she was at Chris's house because of the fight. I was afraid I'd be blamed for her death. I was already blaming myself. My inner turmoil found its expression in destructive ways through my teen years as I began to steal, drink, and lie.

Later I would learn this is one of the ways kids cope with buried or unresolved grief. If they can't act it out honestly, they will act it out dishonestly. And unless there is a way for us as children to safely express our grief, we will carry it into our adulthood. Grief is held in our psyche and our body, seeping out in unhealthy ways until the day it surfaces so strongly that we must face it and come to terms with it. My grief had long been forgotten. Now, with a secret I felt I had to preserve at all costs and the impending loss of my marriage, I was facing grief as an adult. And as I began to cry for the first time since the day I learned of Susan's murder, the floodgates opened and myriad emotions overtook me. In my panic, I moved out one morning after Bill left for work.

> *I moved into my new place last week, a one-room in-law unit on Walnut Street in North Berkeley. I am relieved to be alone with my thoughts, my things, and with time to sort everything out. As I was unpacking yesterday, I came across a white linen fabric with white embroidery that my Nana, Marianna Cacciatore, crocheted. I didn't want to look for a special place for it so I placed it on a shelf. Later my friend Homer came over to see my new place and to take me to dinner. Looking around, he said, "I see you've created an altar."*

> *Homer pointed over my shoulder. I turned and there, behind me, was a single shelf on a white wall with my Nana's white linen cloth draped over it. On top of the cloth was a melange of treasured objects I had unpacked and put aside—Susan's photo, a shell from Stinson Beach, several feathers I'd collected over the years, and a rounded stone from a trip to Yosemite. They*

looked as though they had been arranged just so, yet I had no such thought when I placed them.

Stunned, I felt like I was seeing a mirage. My Nana was there with Susan and a cluster of treasures in a reverential display. Something deeply within had been conspiring to create this. What do I do now?

Choosing to Heal

I remember the night Susan disappeared how scared I was that she would return after we had gone to bed; after we had turned out all the lights. Even though we left the lights on in the house that night, we turned the lights off within ourselves. Me, my parents, everyone I knew were going about their lives as though the most horrible atrocity had not taken place in our midst. Now, as I began the work of unraveling layers of protection, I was finally making a conscious choice to leave the light on within me. I began to see a therapist.

I simply cannot stop crying. I cry in restaurants, in bed, at the library, walking down the street. I had no idea I had this much sorrow and grief inside of me. My friends are worried. They've never seen me like this. The other day an old friend said, "Marianna, I count on you to be the strong one. Now look at you." I lost my composure and screamed that it wasn't fair to make the strong one always the strong one. I will not agree to it. I am falling apart and I have a right to! Later we had a gin and tonic and laughed. It felt good to finally laugh a little.

I see my therapist once a week and it is hardly enough. So I write day and night and won't venture out without my journal. I have no choice now but to let it out. It feels like a purging of pain long held, a bit wild and uncontrolled. I wake up with so many things in my head that need to be said. The most remarkable thing to me is how the grief from fourteen years ago was frozen inside until I was ready to render it thawed. Pushing it down, "making it go black," did not make it go away.

Thank God for Homer. He's a new friend I met in the park—a Buddhist monk who, for seventeen years, has been living at Tassahara, an ashram near Big Sur. Grief and death are topics he seems to understand and talk about in an easy way. I can cry, laugh, and say just about anything to him and he listens well. I don't feel so broken afterward.

Being a Companion

Just like Homer, we all have the capacity to embrace the suffering of someone else. Being a companion takes a willing heart and a desire to soften and surrender our fierce need to rescue the ones we love. The painful spectrum of emotions we call grief won't destroy us. In truth, holding grief back is more dangerous. When we construct a barrier to keep the grief away, that same barrier imprisons us and we lose connection with our inner compass, as I had after fourteen years of repressed grief. Homer did not try to rescue me from my sorrow. He let me be.

At some time each of us will need to midwife someone we love through their grief. At another time we will need to be held through ours. In life we take turns loving, grieving, and holding each other along the way. And we learn to do this by doing it, by courageously facing the sorrows as well as the joys of life, even when it brings up our own painful emotions.

✳ Being Deeply Present

Our collective purpose on earth is to love, to learn to love and care for one another. And it is the greatest risk we ever take. Love demands nothing less than our complete vulnerability. Ask any parent of a seriously ill child about the pain and powerlessness of knowing their child could die soon.

None of us ever know when our loved ones will die, so I urge you to make the commitment—right here, right now—to love well.

How do we love and care for one another? There are many ways, but one way—one critical, yet simple, way—is to be deeply present to your loved ones so they can honestly express themselves and come to know who they are. So they can flourish!

Being deeply present means I am nowhere but here. I offer my unhurried attention. I listen to you, I see you, I accept you, I have faith in your wholeness. In this moment I am not focused on myself, I am not shifting the conversation to me, I am not thinking of how to fix you. I am not projecting forward or remembering the past, I have no agenda, I am here for you. In this precious moment, I see you.

It takes a lifetime to learn to do this well.

Most of us are afraid to journey into darker territory, but the only way to reach the other side is "through." The road is not straight, nor is it always clear, but we are never alone. It has been journeyed by many.

Being a companion takes persistent willingness to learn to listen, which sometimes involves a commitment to look within. It asks us to let go of our judgments and preconceived notions of how our loved one "should" be grieving. Listening generously means letting go of any expectations we have. It invites us to trust the process. Homer understood this and must have had faith that I would heal. I felt it and it helped me to have faith in myself.

Although Homer was a blessing to me, he was a friend I saw only occasionally. I was still crying more hours in a day than I ever thought was humanly possible. I am sure if my family had known the full truth of my emotional life, they would have intervened in some way. But they were in Tucson and I was in California and it was easy to hide.

It's 2 pm and I just remembered a dream I had last night or early this morning. Thank God I didn't remember it till now. It would have scared me to death if I had recalled it while still in bed. I feel so fragile. The past three days I have been obsessed with how Susan died, how she felt, if she had been raped. My crying has felt hysterical.

In the dream I saw Susan's murderer at my bedside with his arms raised above his head and a hatchet in his hand. He swung his arms down and I panicked for a second—one second—then the hatchet landed at the crown of my head and split my skull in two. The very next second I felt peace, a deep, unshakable peace. Now as I'm remembering the dream, it feels like Susan has given me a gift. Maybe she only suffered for one second. Maybe in death she feels that kind of peace all the time.

In time I left California and found my way to Tucson, where most of my family resided. Eventually I reentered therapy and learned to meditate, a practice that would one day come to be the tool that helped me the most in my work with grieving adults.

Thus our sorrow becomes our gift. From within our tender hurt there can spring kindness, generosity, and love for others. In our grief and confusion, we may mistakenly believe we have no offering to bring the family of the earth. But mere suffering cannot extinguish the priceless gift of our true nature. As soon as we begin to heal—the instant we experience some degree of inner clarity or spaciousness—in the very next breath, generosity naturally arises. As we feel the measure of our own strength, we simultaneously experience a natural impulse to share it. This is not faith, this is simple spiritual physics: As we are fed, so do we wish to feed others.

—Wayne Muller, *How Then Shall We Live?*

4
The SALT in Tears

I N 1988 my sorrow, and my healing, had found its next path, creating a place where young people who were grieving would have someone to talk to as close to the time of the death as possible. I suppose I wanted to give kids the help I didn't get. I wanted to help other parents learn how to help their children through the maze of feelings that kids experience when someone has died. I imagined a whole community—my community—in which grief was a household word instead of a hidden thing. A place where everyone understood that grief, in its purest form, was simply an expression of love for the one who died. In the end, I wanted to do something that would honor Susan and her family, something that would bring the tragedy of her death full circle.

I envisioned a beautiful homelike atmosphere, a place where people of all ages would find companionship around their loss, rooms where kids talked and played with other kids who had experienced the death of someone they loved, rooms where adults could share their stories of loss with one another. So I founded Children to Children, a program where children and the adults in their lives could find comfort and relief. We began in donated space at a local church in Arizona, where I was living. Later, a friend, Alice Belmonte, purchased a beautiful 3,000-square-foot historic home on an acre of land and donated it to the Tucson Community Foundation for our exclusive use.

From my journal:

Our first group in the new building was remarkable last night. The depth of sharing among the adults went far deeper than it ever had at the church. The same was true in the kids' group. There is something about "place" that impacts communication. I was right to light the adult room with floor lamps that softly illuminate. The cozy couches and chairs were helpful too— so different than the folding chairs and bright lighting at the church.

The kids' rooms are loaded with bright, primary-colored pillows and stuffed animals. All of our volunteers showed up last night—one adult for every two kids—and they all sat on the pillows for the talking circle. The Volcano Room was a big hit. The playground isn't ready yet. It was hard to keep the energy contained inside, but the art table helped.

Anyone Can Learn by Heart

At Children to Children, we reached out to our community for volunteers to be trained, and over the years hundreds—thousands by now—came forward to learn about grief and how to gaze into the face of suffering without turning away or *trying* to fix it. Together, as we listened to people's stories, we watched them do their work. And one by one, they healed.

We provided support, not therapy. In teaching people how to offer support, we primarily used one aspect of what a good therapist would do: listening.

Lay people can be very instrumental in helping others traverse the journey of grief. In fact, if they are well trained to listen generously and not cross the boundary into therapy, they will, with utmost integrity, offer the invaluable gift of their deep presence, which is very therapeutic.

In teaching, I created an acronym to help *learn by heart* four basic premises for support. It speaks to **the SALT in Tears.**

See them.
Allow them.
Listen to them.
Trust them.

- **See them:** If you can simply see someone in grief without acting on the urge to alter or fix that person in some way, it allows them the freedom to uncover *their own* strength, resilience, and creative responses to life. For one who is grieving, being seen validates and makes real their experiences, which is a powerful force for healing. To see someone in sorrow and be calmly present with that person is quite possibly the most valuable skill you will learn in a lifetime—for the one who is grieving and for yourself.

- **Allow them:** Each person grieves differently. They may say or do things that are out of character for them. Allow them this freedom (as long as they don't hurt themselves

31

or another). Don't add your fear or criticism. Compassion is the most helpful and healing gift you can offer. Acceptance of another in this unpredictable time of sorrow will permeate the membrane of self-acceptance as well. As it flourishes, so do you.

- **Listen to them:** If they need to talk for a while and they choose to do it with you, listen generously. Don't interrupt. Don't give advice. Let them know you are hearing them through your eye contact, a nod, a sigh. Learn to breathe deeply and allow silence to be part your exchange. Give them all the space and time they need to let the deeper words come to the surface and be spoken—and sometimes there are no words. Your presence itself is enough to qualify as generous listening. And as you learn to quiet your busy mind and simply listen to another, you'll also begin to hear the still, small voice within yourself—the voice of your inner wisdom.

- **Trust them:** Within us lies everything we need to heal. Given any kind of safe and nurturing environment, we move toward healing. Your role is to provide that safe haven for the person you care about, and have faith in their inherent resilience. If you can trust this process and their unique journey, your faith will make them stronger and help them to have faith in themselves, if only a morsel, even in their darkest hour. And I encourage you to trust your own process as well. You have the capacity to embrace the sorrow of another, and to remain fully present through it all. I promise you.

See them.
Allow them.
Listen to them.
Trust them.

A friend who can be silent with us in a moment of despair or confusion, who can stay with us in an hour of grief or bereavement, not curing, not healing, and face with us the reality of our powerlessness, that is a friend who cares.

—Henri Nouwen, *Out of Solitude*

5
See Them

PAMELA WAS a thin, fairy-like ten-year-old girl with one long blond braid that swung down her back. She had been a happy-go-lucky child until a car accident forever changed her life. Traveling in the car with her parents, she was the only one to survive. Her grandmother brought her to the Dougy Center in Portland, Oregon, the place where I received my training in grief support. Pamela had become quite despondent, falling behind in school, losing weight, and growing more pale with each passing day. She was withdrawing from life. Each week she attended the sessions, but didn't participate. She only watched.

One evening the program director, Izetta Smith, spotted Pamela alone in one of the playrooms dancing in front of a mirror. Izetta quietly took two steps into the room and sat on the floor to watch. She was careful not to step too far into the room or speak. Izetta was an observer, and she was testing the waters. Would Pamela let her stay? Did Pamela *want* her to watch?

Pamela saw Izetta enter the room. She continued dancing for several minutes, then stopped and left without a word.
The following week, the young girl shyly approached Izetta
and motioned for her to follow. She led Izetta to the same
room and pointed to the floor where she wanted Izetta to sit.
This time Pamela danced with more abandon. Her closure was
exactly the same—without notice, she would stop dancing and
leave the room without a word. For several weeks she repeated this ritual, but each time the dance was longer and wilder.
Eventually, Pamela was dancing so intensely that she would
be completely sweaty by the end of the evening. No conversations ever took place, just the wildly feverish dancing.

One evening as the support group was ending, Pamela's
grandmother told Izetta that Pamela was participating again
in schoolwork. She was eating more, and color was returning
to her cheeks. She thanked Izetta: "I don't know what you're
doing in there, but whatever it is, it's working."

What Izetta was "doing in there" was watching, with respectful acceptance, Pamela's unique expression of grief. For
Pamela, the power of simply being seen was the healing balm
she needed. The work was hers to do. At ten years old she knew
that, and she knew she could not do it alone. Luckily, so did
Izetta. Had Izetta failed to understand the foreign language of
Pamela's healing journey of grief, she might have missed the
opportunity to offer help in the way it was most needed. Izetta
had faith that Pamela knew how to heal, and she honored her
by bearing witness to this expression of grief—her dance! In
being seen, Pamela *felt* herself again. Her life was here, on
earth, in her body. She began to eat again, to talk and laugh
again, to engage again in life.

THE SAFE CONTAINER

Recounting Pamela's story brings to mind a dream I had several years ago:

I am living on a houseboat. It is nighttime. From a bird's-eye view, I can see myself sleeping in the berth, curled up under my down comforter. There is a big storm. The boat is rocking feverishly from side to side. From deep under the water come two large hands that are nearly the length of the boat itself. They are positioned on either side of the boat, not quite touching it, but clearly lending support. When the boat rocks to the left, the hands move to the left. When the boat rocks to the right, the hands move to the right.

To me, these are the hands of a friend who understands the power of simply being present for another person, seeing them without needing to fix anything or rescue anyone. There is no intervention to stop the feverish rocking, which represents *my work yet to do.* My friend is not there to take my work away and make it all better. Rather, my friend is there to bear witness to my turmoil and to support and assure me that I am not alone. The hands move *with me* to the rhythm of my tumultuous life in this moment. My friend, my companion, creates a "container" for my grief, and I feel stronger and more resilient as a result. I have faith in myself, in my ability to heal.

The Buddha said that life is filled with ten thousand joys and ten thousand sorrows. In the depths of grief, people can feel they are experiencing the ten thousand sorrows all at once. Our job is to create a "safe container" in which they can heal. But the healing work is theirs. They must work through grief themselves, just as children must learn to walk by

37

themselves. Whatever they feel, whatever they do, is theirs. They do it for their own well-being, in order to inhabit their own life. If we try to take their sorrow away, or redirect them in some way, we do them a disservice. The safe container we create is an invisible, but deeply felt, touchstone that reassures them—at a very primal level—they won't disappear, or lose their mind, or experience any other "out of control" thing they might imagine in the midst of their ten thousand sorrows. Izetta's safe container allowed Pamela to dance, timidly at the start and with wild abandon at the end.

The Pace of Seeing

Sometimes in order to really see someone, we must slow down and adjust our eyes to the "pace of seeing." I remember traveling often to a beach house in Mexico that my husband and I rented for a year when we were living in Tucson. I was working full time as executive director of Children to Children and often could only arrange one extra day tacked on to an occasional weekend. After several trips, a pattern emerged: We would leave on Thursday night after work and arrive at 10 pm. Friday was spent unloading the car, going to town for food, setting up the canopy on the beach, going for a run, and writing a few letters. Saturday was similar, not quite as busy, but we were still running around. We would go to town for a fabulous *huevos rancheros* breakfast; stop at a few shops on the way back to the beach house; maybe go for a run when we got back. You get the picture. On Sunday morning we would finally wake up feeling slow and easy. The rhythm of the tide had registered somewhere deeper than a sound in our ears. The last thing we wanted to do was get in the car and drive to town. It was a day of deeper conversations, long naps on the beach, lovemaking, eating, and laughter. The point is this: Even in the best of conditions, moving from a fast pace to a slow one takes time.

As a friend to someone who is grieving, consciously slowing down is helpful if you want to be more present. I am not suggesting that you take three days off before spending time with a grieving friend. I am inviting you into a conscious relationship with the pace at which you move and your own deeper rhythms.

BREATHING IN A SYNCHRONOUS RHYTHM

Sharon Salzberg, a Buddhist meditation teacher, told me a story about visiting her friend Alan who was recovering from surgery in a hospital. After their initial greetings, she sat down in the chair next to Alan's bed and, in their small talk, she began to take note of the pace of her breath. In the silences between their talking, she noticed the pace of Alan's breathing as well. Soon her breath moved into synchronous rhythm with his, the pace set by her friend. They related this way for several minutes, quietly communicating a deep connection and love—a sharing that went much deeper than speaking, a communion beneath words.

A few minutes later a group of relatives arrived. Suddenly people were filling the room with words, getting him water, helping him to sit up. The pace shifted to that of the visitors. Alan, who had no energy to ask for what he needed in the face of so much well-intentioned chaos, simply did the best he could to be present with his guests. The moment was gone.

The kind of communication occurring between Sharon and Alan is subtle and deep, requiring us to place our attention on the inner self with a movement toward stillness. We

Deep Presence

Every one of us is whole and complete.

Within us lie the answers to every question we have, the quandaries we find ourselves in, the doubts we cannot reconcile. We know which way to go, when to stop, and when to lead. But we forget.

Remembering, whether for ourselves or helping another to remember, requires our unhurried, gentle presence. This has been true since time began and will likely be true forever. However, we will not come to know our truth if we move too fast. We must go slow.

We sometimes get a glimpse of our deepest self on Sunday mornings in bed with our lover, in the nightlight-talk we have while tucking our child into bed, or in an honest conversation with someone who doesn't need to prove anything to anyone anymore.

The speed of things, and the filling of every nanosecond with sound, threatens these moments. When nothing around us is quiet, we lose our tolerance for silence. When everything comes to us so fast, we become impatient with things that move slowly. But, as I said, our deepest presence has been here since time began and will be here forever. It does not go away. It's just a little harder to find.

drop into a place beneath all the pillow fluffing, beneath all the chatter, beneath the anxiety that tiptoes away from feelings of loss, sorrow, grief, and depression.

If Sharon and Alan had been able to continue their inner communion, it might have progressed into a conversation about matters of the heart. Human beings are given a voice that grants us the ability to say aloud all that we feel within, to have a forum in which we can hear our life speak, a voice that is our access to a life larger than us. When we are in fear, grief or despair, having someone who can stay and bear witness—to be still and silent, to listen as we fumble through words and feelings—gives us access to a road that had been hidden, a path of healing.

What I have learned, and what I remember on a good day, is that there is a way to care for someone that is aligned with *their* rhythm—a way that offers our presence with acceptance of where *they are.* It is not always easy but it can be learned. And if we stay, we are honored to witness the incredible resiliency in people. We come to see they have everything they need inside of them. We learn their journey is as unique as their fingerprint. In time we become more flexible about our differences, more willing to let things go the way the river is flowing, more aware of the deeper mystery and precise timing that permeates our world. It fills out our humanness and balances our ego. We come to see one another with softer eyes, our common humanity laid before us. The things that separate us begin to melt away.

Do you remember a time when you moved more slowly— perhaps on vacation, even if it was only for a day or a weekend? Were you at the beach, toes in the warm sand, listening to the sound of sea gulls in the distance, feeling the pull of the tide? Was it a walk in the woods, listening to the wind in the trees, feeling the earth below your feet? Maybe it was during a meditation or a time of quiet contemplation. We slow our pace so we can observe the world from a quieter, more compassionate place within us; so we can adjust our eyes to the "pace of seeing." In our newfound spaciousness, we simply see the one we love and make room for them to walk through their grief, letting them teach us about their journey. We listen with our full attention. And we trust they will heal. We begin creating a safe container for their trek as well as ours.

Hearing the Roses

One night at Children to Children, Karen, a parent in our grief support group whose husband, John, had recently died, took the talking stick: "I dreamt of John last Thursday night and I have not told this dream to anyone. We were in our garden and he asked me if I could hear the roses grow. I said I couldn't. He said, 'Listen. Be really still and listen.' I tried as hard as I could, but I couldn't hear them. He turned to me and said, 'It takes time. You have to practice. I can hear them every day now.'" She said to us: "I woke up in the dark and turned on my bedside lamp to get a tissue, and there, on my nightstand, was a vase with three roses from our garden I had placed there the afternoon before. I felt as though the roses had spoken to me through the dream and I had heard them."

Karen was crying as she spoke. She had also been fingering the fringe on the end of the talking stick. Now she laid it down in her lap. No one moved or spoke. Her presence in the room was palpable even without her speaking. She had our full attention. We were holding her within the safe container of our group. And she cried more deeply. Finally, when she

42

The Talking Stick

Passing a talking stick is a ritual borrowed from ancient tribal peoples. The talking stick is used to signify who has the floor, yet it is so much more than that. The presence of a talking stick creates a sacred mood. It slows things down and creates an environment for listening—including the speaker's listening to their own inner emotions and feelings.

The basic guidelines for using a talking stick are simple: Sit in circle, if you can. Whoever has the stick speaks; whoever doesn't, listens. Speak and listen from your heart. When speaking, stay focused on yourself. When listening, stay focused on the speaker. Be deeply present for them, try not to wander. Don't plan ahead what you are going to say. Practice trusting yourself—your inner wisdom—to say just the right thing at the right time. Allow for silence; it has much to teach us. No interrupting or advice-giving is allowed. Anyone who chooses not to speak can pass.

was finished, she looked up and said, "I miss him so much. But since then, since that dream, I am strangely comforted. I think he was telling me that he is at a place of beauty, where he can even hear the roses grow. Now when I want to be with him, I work in my garden. I can feel him there."

Karen held the talking stick in her hand long after she had finished speaking. We all sat in silence. It was as though her feelings were being revered like a Monet painting in a gallery. Her telling of this significant dream rested in our hearts like a weary traveler who had finally found a warm, soft bed for the night. We were her companions on this journey of healing. To whom else could she have told this story and shared the feeling of it in awe and silence? We had been creating a safe container over a period of months together, and she trusted us.

Our work as companions to someone in grief is to learn to listen deeply and allow periods of silence to occur. We learn to simply see someone as they are and bear witness to their story, their experience, their dream, their dance, their life. In these silences the new realities in the grieving person's life slowly surface and find their place. This deep work is all-encompassing to them.

Noticing the Cue

In our group with Karen, the talking stick alerted all of us to be quiet and simply pay attention, but in normal conversation there is no talking stick. I was hiking the other day with my friends Helen and Judy. As we began the trek, Judy said, "I don't know how long I'm going to last on this hike. I was up half the night with my daughter, Sarah, and I'm tired. The minute I would drift off to sleep, she would wake up crying. Joe and I alternated getting up, but every time it was my turn, I had just fallen asleep. By morning, I was irritable with Sarah *and* Joe. Sarah has an ear infection. Joe and I have sleep deprivation. And all I can think of is that I wish my mom was here."

Helen chimed in: "I remember when Robin was that young. She was such a restless baby. I swear she didn't sleep through the night till she was three years old. And she hardly ever took naps. She would call for us all night, even when she wasn't sick. She just wanted company! I remember one time when we were all leaving on a trip in the morning. It was an early flight, and Robin kept us up all night. We arrived at my sister's house for the holidays looking like zombies. We walked in the front door, gave the baby to my sister, went directly to the guest bedroom, and fell sound asleep at 4:30 in the afternoon. My sister was great. She didn't wake us up for dinner or anything, and we slept till 9 that night. We simply passed out. But, you know, these kids grow out of it. In no time, Sarah will be sleeping from 8 till 8. Young kids really need 10–12 hours. It won't be long, she'll be sleeping through the night."

Later that day in a phone conversation with Judy, I discovered that this day was the two-year anniversary of her mother's death. On our walk that morning, Judy had *tiptoed* into deeper waters by saying, "and all I can think of is that I wish my mom was here."

Quite often, the last thing someone says is a cue to a deeper feeling that is longing for expression. But only when we are fully present for the conversation can we hear it.

On our morning walk, Judy needed someone who could listen to her. Had we been silent after she made the comment about her mom, leaving an opening for her to go deeper, she might have touched on the issue that was just below the story of her sleepless night: that it was the anniversary of her mother's death. In the moment we notice the cue, one thing we can privately do is imagine that the person we're with is holding a talking stick in her hand. We can stop our busy mind and quietly become a curious student, inviting her to teach us about her grief. Most likely, she will never consciously know we've made a shift—however, she will feel it on a deeper level.

Another thing we could have done was ask a question, not to satisfy our curiosity, but to let her know that her comment about her mom had been heard and to convey an invitation to say more. "What would your mom have done if she were here?" Judy might have begun at once, talking about her mom. Or perhaps she would have been silent for a while before speaking. Considering that she was so tired, she might have begun to cry. Anything is possible, but whatever might have happened would have been Judy's story, not Helen's.

We frequently respond to someone's tale by telling our own story because this is a common way to "make conversation" in our culture. With conscious effort, though, we can notice when we're doing it, stop, take a deep breath, and imagine a talking stick in their hand. With our exhalation, we can offer up a moment of compassion for our companion, and for ourselves.

In grief, uncertainty permeates the landscape. Everything seems different. A grieving person doesn't know where they'll land. But what is foundationally true is that *each person must feel their own feelings in their own order, in their own time.* They do not need us to pull their attention away from their inner process to listen to our stories. Rather, they need us to give them the few things they cannot give themselves: a safe container, our non-intrusive attention, our faith in their ability to traverse this road. In time, they will come to accept the reality of their loss. But *how* they get to this acceptance will be unique. If we can be present and awake, listen well, and put our own story aside for now, in time they will heal and we will be honored to witness their journey of deepening and healing. If we can offer up even a moment of compassion for ourselves and for our companion as they explore the territory of grief, we will have done the therapeutic equivalent of something as monumental as a walk on the moon!

The people who help us grow toward true self offer unconditional love, neither judging us to be deficient nor trying to force us to change but accepting us exactly as we are. And yet this unconditional love does not lead us to rest on our laurels. Instead, it surrounds us with a charged force field that makes us want to grow from the inside out—a force field that is safe enough to take the risks and endure the failures that growth requires.

—Parker Palmer, *A Hidden Wholeness*

6
Allow Them

Jimmy's eyes were wide open as he moved from room to room during his intake visit at Children to Children, yet he never left his mother's side and often asked to be held. He was small for his age, very smart, and we could tell he had a heightened sense of awareness about the world and his surroundings. At four years old, he had been through a lot. His father had just died of a brain tumor and, thirteen months earlier, his only brother, died of Sudden Infant Death Syndrome (SIDS). His family had gone from four people to two at a time in his life when he was just forming his ideas about how the world works.

At Children to Children, our evening programs typically place the adults in a different setting than the children or teens. On Jimmy's first night, however, he had another plan in mind. He had been enamored with the Volcano Room when he came for his intake interview and he wanted to go there now. Furthermore, he wanted his mom with him. We explained that we had other plans for the evening and that he could go to the Volcano Room later. He insisted on doing it his way. There was something uniquely intense in his persistence and the quality of the interaction that prompted our program director, Teresiana Zurita, to restructure the evening and give him what he seemed to need and was having no trouble communicating.

THE VOLCANO ROOM

The Volcano Room, a special place for what we called "big feelings," has red walls made of dense foam covered in fabric so we can bounce our body against them and not hurt ourselves. In the center is a cube the size of a low dresser, also made of foam and covered in red fabric. In the corner of the room are an array of "bats" and things to hit with. Some are wrapped in foam and fabric while others are shaped like swords and made of a flexible yet firm but very lightweight foam material. Around the perimeter of the room are big pillows and brightly covered futons—soft, cushy things to flop on after the kids have exhausted themselves.

Three kids can "work" in this room at a time as long as they have an adult facilitator with them. They select the bat of their choice and begin to hit the cube. They laugh, scream, and yell as loud as they like and as long as they want. They banter with the bats and even hit one another as long as the kids are about the same size and strength, all agree that it's OK, and promise to never hit above the neck. If anyone feels unsafe, they yell, "Stop and I mean it!" And everyone freezes. The facilitator is actively with them the whole time. It's another setting in which to "see" the grieving person as they are and to create a safe container for them to do their work. With kids, that work is very different than with adults—it's active, kinetic, less wordy. Kids are in their bodies.

There is always a group waiting to use the Volcano Room. We tell them that anger is a natural emotion. It's not something to be ashamed of, put aside, or tuck away. At the same time, it doesn't feel good to have anger in our body for very long, so we want to do something with it. We want to move it out because living with it isn't wise or healthy. Anger is such a powerful emotion to express that we created a safety rule to be honored at Children to Children and to be practiced in our lives. *It is not OK to hurt ourselves or other people, or destroy things with our actions or words.* Using the Volcano Room is a healthy way to manage our anger and not hurt anyone in the process.

Playing Dead

When Jimmy, his mother, Deborah, and Teresiana entered the room, Jimmy immediately picked up two play swords. He held one himself and gave the other to his mom. She took it and played with him, all the while allowing him to lead the play. Deborah was following his directives when suddenly he pretended to stab her in the heart and said, "And now you're dead." She immediately turned to Teresiana with a private look of panic. Teresiana nodded for her to continue following his lead. Despite whatever feelings Deborah might have been having, she obliged, falling to the floor and playing dead. Jimmy stood over her with the sword on her chest, and for a while no words were spoken. After a very long minute, he pulled the sword away and said, "And now you're alive."

Deborah got up and Jimmy began playing again, bantering back and forth with the sword. She again followed his lead. Once again, Jimmy "stabbed" her and pronounced her dead. She fell to the floor and quietly lay there as he surveyed his "corpse." A minute later he brought her back to life and they resumed their play.

51

This went on for a while with several episodes of dying and returning to life. Deborah completely adapted her rhythm to Jimmy's, allowing the play and the tempo to be all his, no matter what painful emotions she must have been feeling inside. When Jimmy finally felt finished, he laid the sword down and reached up for his mom to hold him. She picked him up and sat down on the large red cube in the middle of this padded Volcano Room. He curled into his mother's arms and began to cry. She held him and cried as well. The silent permission she now gave by crying *with* him allowed Jimmy the added safety he needed to go to the bottom of his feelings. He sobbed more heavily.

Deborah and Teresiana allowed Jimmy what he needed that night. They played curious student to his role as teacher. They believed that Jimmy had his own wisdom to know what he needed to heal from his losses. If they had not been so faithful to this truth, they might have done or said something that would have stopped him from expressing his anguish, sorrow, and fear that his mother would also die. Instead they allowed Jimmy to do what he needed to do to heal his broken heart. Deborah courageously matched her moment-to-moment rhythm to her son's. She played his sword game on his terms. She listened. She participated. She saw her son and accepted his journey that night. She did not try to take his pain away so that she could feel better. Nor did she communicate disapproval. She felt fearful for a moment, but Teresiana's simple gesture of encouragement was all she needed to go on with it. It was a magical night in which Deborah and Teresiana created a safe container for Jimmy, allowing him to go where he needed to go. He was given a gift that offered him the freedom to heal and to grow. Deborah, in the exchange, received the very same gift.

JUST HOLD SPACE

I remember receiving a telephone call from a man named Sergio whose wife had died a month previously in an automobile accident. Their baby daughter, Carmela, was only six months old. Typically, Carmela had been a quiet and happy child who slept easily. Since her mother's death, however, she had cried without consolation and awakened often. Her father asked if it was possible she was grieving. Rather than answer directly, I replied with a question: "Do you think Carmela loved her mother?"

"Yes," he said without hesitation.

"So, if she is old enough to love, then wouldn't it make sense that she is old enough to grieve?" I asked. "At this age, children experience life through their senses. Carmela misses the smell of her mother, the feel of her skin, the sound of her voice, even the rhythm of your wife's heartbeat. The attachments that are made *in utero* are at the very core of our being. It would be odd if Carmela did *not* grieve such a significant loss."

Even though our groups for children start at three years old, I invited Sergio to meet with me for an hour with Carmela. When they arrived we talked for a while. I could see that Sergio was a tender and loving father who was simply perplexed about how to help his daughter. Carmela was a beautiful child with dark skin and curly black hair. She clung to her father but was fidgety. When she began to cry, Sergio tried to calm her by walking around my office, heavily patting her on the back, rocking her up and down and saying, "There, there, it's OK." Carmela continued to squirm and then started to sob.

I suggested that perhaps she *needed* to cry. Could he stop patting her on the back and trying to get her to stop? Could he, instead, hold Carmela close to his chest with a solid grip, not to squeeze her, but to hold her with a sense of stillness and security? With his words he could tell her, "I am here for you. I'm sorry Mommy died. I miss her too. *I* love you and *I* am here."

We spent another hour together talking, and after they left I wondered what would happen. As his daughter expresses her grief, will Sergio be able to allow Carmela her journey and bear witness to her sorrow? Will he be present and still through it? Will he create a safe container for her? Will he slow down and become silent within himself so that he can be fully available for Carmela with no agenda? Learning to "hold space" for someone who is grieving is a heroic act of generosity that requires courage and fortitude. Yet we don't have to feel heroic or courageous as we start. In fact, most of us don't even feel confident as we embark on the journey. We simply start where we are and make a commitment to stay.

THE RHYTHM OF LIFE

In my own life, when I was in sixth grade, I could see Susan Brady's house from my classroom window. After she disappeared, and before they found her body, I sat staring at it every day. No one talked about her anymore. It was bizarre. I could think of nothing else. When we would say our morning prayers at school, Sister Lenore included Susan and her family, but that was the only time any of the adults in my life mentioned her—at school or at home.

On Valentine's Day I looked up from my desk and across the field to Susan's house beyond it to find six cars parked in a row. It was rare to see any cars there at all, and today there were six! *She's home! It's Valentine's Day and she's home!* I just knew it.

I raced home for lunch, across the sports field, through the cul-de-sac, and up my street. Out of breath, I ran into the house and found my mom sitting in the living room listening to the radio. I could hardly contain myself. "Mom, I saw cars in front of Susan's. What's going on? She's home. I know it! It's Valentine's Day! She came home finally. Can I see her? Can I go over there?"

My mother was quiet, deliberate, as she looked at me with forlorn eyes. She turned off the radio and asked me to sit down. I was breathing heavy and fast from running home and was too excited to sit, but I did. Mom wasn't smiling, but I knew Susan was home. I figured my mom didn't know it yet. She hadn't seen the cars in front of Susan's house, but I had.

And then she said, "Honey, they did find Susan, but she's dead. They didn't find her, they found *her body*."

At the word *body,* a roaring sound filled my head and it was louder than my mom's voice. Her lips were moving. I was panicked. My heart was racing even faster now and I strained to pay attention. To hear what I didn't want to hear.

I kept blinking my eyes as though I could keep the tears from coming, as though the next time I opened them, the scene would be different, the story would have changed, the words I was hearing would have gone away.

"I don't know all of what happened," she continued. "The newsman said they found parts of her body in someone's garage. They found other parts in an incinerator."

The roaring in my head burst through and I couldn't hear any more words. Everything was red. My mother, the room, the radio, my feet. I was screaming and my legs were running, running. Instinctively I knew I needed to stay inside my home. I knew I needed the contained space of my house, the walls, the floor, the ceiling. Outside, I would split into a million little pieces and never come back together again.

I landed in my bedroom and curled into a ball on my bed, getting very small and solid. I held myself together, screaming and crying, pressing my hands to my ears as though I could block out what I'd already heard. As though I could stop it from being true.

My mother was with me and yet I was alone. She sat on the side of my bed and rubbed my back as I sobbed. I could feel her body and her hand but I could not feel her. I suppose she didn't know how to handle this kind of trauma. Perhaps she thought if she cried with me, she might fall apart herself. I don't know. I only know I felt alone. Susan was dead and I was very, very alone.

Parents generally think that, in order to convey strength, they cannot cry in the presence of their children. It isn't true. We do our children a disservice by pretending to be stoic when we are sad. As the adult in their life, we can *show* our children an honest response to the painful things that happen. In traversing the land of sorrow together for awhile, we show our children how life really is—that hard things happen; that we may have strong feelings when they do; that strong emotions subside in time; it won't stay like this forever. We can show them through our actions, and tell them with our words, that when someone dies, it's hard to say goodbye, no matter how old we are; that tears are helpful to shed, and if we feel what there is to feel, and don't resist what comes naturally, we heal in time.

In 1965 there were no support services for my parents; no one guiding them on how to be there for me in this traumatic time. Gratefully, over the years much has changed.

Today, there are services in nearly every city to help parents help their children heal from the immense sorrow that comes when someone they love has died. Go to page 118 for grief support resources.

A PATH TO KNOWING

One morning I woke up after having facilitated a particularly difficult Children to Children support group the night before, and four words came to me, as though from a dream. They are:

> **Silence**
> **Slowing**
> **Breathing**
> **Knowing**

These four simple words were a clear message to slow down, be still, and use my breath to clear the way from uncertainty to knowing. They came as a reminder that I have within me a wisdom, and the way to access that wisdom is more about being than doing. Whatever uncertainty I had the night before about the support group suddenly felt manageable. It didn't go away, but I felt hopeful that if I created a safe container for myself by making time to slow down, be silent, and place my attention on my breath, that a knowing would reveal itself.

For fifteen years now , these four simple words have offered me a path out of my limited thinking and revealed a portal into my deepest knowing. I begin with a meditation to silence my mind. Each time I notice my thoughts returning, I imagine holding them gently in my hands. In front of me I see a bubbling creek and there I lay my burdens down and watch them float out of sight, out of mind. I slow everything down and begin to see—really see—from a deeper, wiser place within me. Noticing my breath, I inhale more fully and exhale more slowly. And in time, on some days, my thoughts stop coming so quickly. I am touching on some inner place where my wisdom resides. Here I know that my doubts are just a product of my busy mind. Here I know the truth of who I am and who the other people I care about are. Here I see the brightness of the light within them. I commune with their resilience and I know.

~~~

And still, there are times when we offer our deepest presence and the person in grief doesn't "heal." They seem to remain in a cycle of fear or resentment, or anger. The operative word here is "seem." We are challenged to remove any arrogance that tells us where this person is in their sojourn. We truly have no way of knowing. In such a situation, one of the most difficult things we are called to do is continue to be available and present with no expectation of outcome, offering our compassion for the human condition, for the person we care about. For those who are grieving and unavailable, unwilling to respond, and seemingly unmovable, we must practice letting go. If they are going to move at all, it will only be when they feel the constraint of our expectation gone. We are challenged to be both present and open to any outcome for as long as it takes. It goes without saying this is much more difficult when the person is someone whose day-to-day choices impact our daily life.

Start Where You Are

When we learn to be of service to another without imposing our ideas and advice, eventually the truth of our own wholeness begins to reveal itself.

This is how it works. In the beginning we encourage ourselves to believe in another person's inner strength and offer our deepest presence, even if it is difficult. Over time we see their inner strength come to the surface and they heal. Suddenly it dawns on us that what is true for the person we are caring for may well be true for us. If they have within them everything they need to heal, then perhaps so do we. At once, the roles of giver and receiver disappear. Both are student and teacher, healer and healed. When the day comes that we find ourselves immersed in sorrow, for one reason or another, we will know we have within us all that we need to heal.

Some people have the reverse experience: They begin by learning to care for themselves and something shifts inside. Self love inspires love for others. Compassion is unleashed from within. From this inspired place, they begin to care for others in an intentional way.

I've seen it work both ways, and in the end it doesn't matter where we start. It's that we start. We start where we are.

THE QUARTER TURN

Anna was in high school when her father died in an automobile accident. She came to Children to Children with her mother, Jean Marie. I was facilitating the adult group at the time but when they arrived, and before our group started, I began to engage Anna in conversation, asking where she went to school and what kinds of things she liked to do. Before Anna had a chance to respond, Jean Marie answered for her. Time and again I tried to engage Anna. Each time Jean Marie would intercede. As the night wore on, I could see that Jean Marie talked incessantly, had very high expectations of her fifteen-year-old daughter, gave advice freely to everyone in my group, interrupted people who had the talking stick, and had a voice that sounded like fingernails on a chalkboard. She was single-handedly dismantling the safe container that we had been nurturing for months. I became angry at her brash behavior and arrogant attitude. I wondered how I was going to be accepting of this person. In truth, I entertained visions of pointing to the door and ordering her out of the group, asking her to keep her fingernails off the chalkboard on her way out.

The following day I called several people to ask for help and advice. As time went on, I found ways to respectfully stop Jean Marie when she interrupted people or gave advice. I began reviewing aloud our group rules at the beginning of each session, hoping she might learn to moderate her own behavior. I did more preparation in advance of our evenings together. I searched for qualities in her that were good and I reflected them back to her. Hoping to feel a measure of compassion for her, I learned more about her life story. Still her brash manner was troubling. I struggled with the idea that if I offered my acceptance of her as a person, and just saw her as she was, it would feel as though I were condoning her behavior. I was so caught in this conundrum I wasn't even sure what "offering my acceptance" would look like.

Each evening when our group was finished and the families had gone home, the volunteers met for an hour in a session we called *post group*. This was our time to work through feelings that had surfaced for us that night and release them before going home. Week after week, when the talking stick was handed to me, I spoke mostly of Jean Marie. I struggled with my strong reaction to her behavior. My *intention* was to see her and accept her as she was. This did not mean I would let her interrupt others or give inappropriate advice. Setting boundaries with her was necessary. But my desire to see her without being judgmental seemed impossible to achieve.

One evening after coming home from our group, I went to bed frustrated. That night I had a dream in which there was a recurring experience, repeated each time with a little twist:

I am pondering a problem. My mind is troubled about a relationship I am struggling with. I am caught in a vortex of obsessive thinking when suddenly something outside of my fixated thoughts catches my attention. Is it a sound? A bell? A breeze? I stop. I can't tell if I hear it or feel it. I turn my head a quarter turn to the right. Suddenly there, before me, is an awe-inspiring vista that takes my breath away. There is an azure blue sky and golden hills with emerald-leaved trees in full bloom. It is incredibly beautiful. And then I hear a voice that says to me, "In every moment, this also."

When I woke up I made a cup of tea and sat to think about this vivid dream. What might it be telling me about my

Acceptance:
Becoming Free by Learning to See

As we accept more of everything and everyone—life's ups and downs, people's personalities, our own failings and disappointments—and see things just as they are, we are free to stop matching everything against some picture of how it should be. When we can simply look and see, we are liberated from the tyranny of our internal judgments and criticisms.

problem with Jean Marie? While I struggled with my feelings about her, the dream was saying that in every moment, this beautiful vista is also possible. The dream seemed to be telling me I could both be irritated with Jean Marie and accept her just as she is *at the same time*. With just a quarter turn, I could access an awe-inspiring vista at the same time that I was troubled and fixated on what seemed to be an intractable problem. Was this possible? Was this what my dream was saying? It reminded me of that familiar meditation practice, in which I sit in silence, notice my breath, and clear my mind for as long as I can. When thoughts re-enter and I become aware of them, I imagine myself placing each thought in a gently flowing stream. There my thoughts "flow downstream" and free my mind to be still again. I vowed to try "the quarter turn."

The next time Jean Marie came to group and spoke, I imagined making a quarter turn. There I discovered a river flowing beneath us—my version of the vista in my dream. I called it my *River of Acceptance* and I breathed life into it. My inhalations and exhalations fed the river. It flowed with no obstacles. Meanwhile, as she spoke, I listened. The river didn't seem to detract from our interaction. I was present. Then, each time I felt myself judging her, I placed her words and manner of speaking, as well as my irritation, in the river and let it flow down and away. I did this again and again, until finally, my mood began to mellow. I still found myself noticing her irritating behavior, but I was not so troubled by it. I was sending it down the river.

One evening, several months later, when our group was over and the families were milling around before leaving, Jean Marie asked if we could talk privately. We stepped into my office. "There is something I've been wanting to tell you," she said. "I am learning to love and accept myself and Anna. It's because I feel your acceptance of *me*. I don't really want to be hard on Anna. I want to love and accept her just as she is. I am learning the value of that by being here. Thank you."

I was stunned. She was no longer interrupting and giving advice in group, but whenever she spoke about her life, it seemed very little had changed. But in fact it had. She *felt* my acceptance of her—which was sincere in my heart even though I had only partially achieved it in my mind. It was *real* to Jean Marie. My intention bore fruit. And finally it was real to me.

I stood in awe of the dream, the quarter turn, and the river—and most especially, the subtlety, grace, and beauty of it all.

I worked hard for months around my expectations of Jean Marie and found a creative and unique way to deal with the powerful triggers inside me. Jean Marie also felt this freedom. It gave her a subtle, unspoken permission to move and change. It may seem kind of woo-woo and magical, but the energetics of it are real. And they are felt. I have seen it often, most recently with my own therapist, who practices Jungian therapy. She rarely gave me advice, mostly listened, and sometimes offered a reflection. However, I felt she loved me, and her acceptance was so profound I was free to dislodge things that had been buried inside since early childhood. In one year's time, I did more work than I had done over many years previously with other therapists who spoke often and gave verbal guidance with regularity. I don't mean to imply there is anything wrong with advice from skilled therapists; there were times when I needed behavioral advice and it was appropriate. I only want to highlight the subtle power of quiet

acceptance and the healing influence of simply being seen—
both easy to disregard because they speak with a whisper.

As listeners, if we do our own work, relax our expectations, and be more curious than afraid, we can be a powerful
healing force in the life of another. Paradoxically, then, we
have a deeper and more satisfying experience of living. There
is a breathing into life that enhances the natural flow of
things. In this softer place, we begin to play with all the as-
pects of this bizarre, unique, unpredictable, wild, sorrowful,
and joyful thing we call life.

Being still and silent,
allowing another to emerge,
is a holy experience.
It is the sacred journey of our own emergence.

—Author's poem, 1997

7
Listen to Them

J ANET, A grandmother whose adult daughter had died, had
been coming to our support group at Children to Children
for several months and had shared bits and pieces of her
daughter Marilyn's death. But most evenings, Janet talked
about the exhausting challenges of her new role as "mother"
to her eight-year-old granddaughter. This evening her mood
was different. She was pensive and brooding. I could tell she
had something on her mind. As our circle began, she immediately reached for the talking stick, settled into her chair, and
began to speak about her daughter's slow death from bone
cancer. It didn't take long to see that on this night, she needed
to tell the whole story—a very graphic, seemingly day-by-day
account of how this degenerative disease progressed and how
she had felt along the way. It was as though she was recreating
the long event, this time with a room full of witnesses she had
grown to trust who would accompany her through it. She no
longer wanted to carry it alone.

When I realized what I was hearing from Janet, my heart beat rapidly. I was intimately familiar with my own grief, but new to the work of being with others in their grief. I felt anxious and unsure whether I had the strength to hear this graphic story and still be able to support a group of bereaved adults. But this was my initiation. There was no way out.

TAKE THE FOLLOW

I took a deep breath and listened. I held her gaze when she looked at me. During the long periods of silence between her words, all of us in the support group remained quiet.

My mind wanted to respond with my deepest presence, but my body was reacting to anxiety. I struggled with inner conditioning that told me that in her moments of silence, she expected me to step in and say something helpful and wise. I longed to think of just the right thing to say, something that would comfort her. But, in fact, my training told me not to interrupt—that it was precisely in these moments Janet did not need someone to break the train of her inner thinking and distract her. I should not "take the lead" but rather "take the follow" and be the curious student learning about her journey of grief. Also, because Janet was near the age of my mother, it was easy to imagine myself in the place of her daughter. *What if this happened to me,* I wondered.

To help myself be present, calm, and quiet, I did three things:

I guided my shallow breath into slow, deep inhalations and exhalations, as I had been doing in meditation for several years. This calmed me and slowed my heart. Soon I noticed that my fear as to whether I could hear this painful story abated. Instead, I became focused on Janet. I was present *with her.* No longer was I thinking about my body deteriorating as

68

Marilyn's had. I was listening to Janet, still and calm, no expectations, no judgments, no projections. My steady breath was like a magic elixir emptying my mind, allowing me to listen generously.

I reminded myself that I need not say or do anything to heal Janet of the pain she was feeling. I trusted Janet had everything she needed within her to be in relationship with her sorrow. This was her journey. The best way I could help her was to have faith that she could traverse this road, to bear witness to her capacity to heal. If I listened from my faithful heart, without interrupting her, I would create a safe container for the trek.

I dismissed my fears that others in the group were resentful about Janet's speaking for so long. Our job, as companions in her support group, was to create the vessel of safety for Janet to touch the places within her she needed to touch alone, but which she could not enter alone. She needed us to listen and to bear witness to her story. We were all learning how to offer our presence. Once I calmed my mind, I knew in my heart that everyone was listening to her and wanted nothing different. We were her companions and we were on holy ground. Everyone knew it.

We felt Janet's broken heart. Many of us gently cried along with her. During those long, deep silences, she gained the courage to continue with her story and told us about the bedside vigil that went on for months, her daughter's steadily diminishing body, her granddaughter's pain and confusion, and, finally, the last moments of her daughter's life.

The companion's role is to "hold" our friend in a way that is long on compassion and free of our own discomfort, whether it's judgment, anxiety, fear, whatever. Most of the time when we are feeling discomfort, we're too "in it" to name it in

A True Companion

Although there are things to learn about *form* when we are with someone in grief, there is no *formula,* because people grieve uniquely, in their own way. Sometimes they want company. Sometimes they need to be alone. At times they are angry; other times, depressed. Grief is very dynamic. To be a companion who can be there through it all, we are asked to slow down and listen for what *they* need, through grief's many faces. All the "helping" or "advice giving" only creates more noise. In fact, to consider your advice or opinion, unless it is explicitly asked for, often requires too much strength for the griever. Your needs are not their needs. Your opinions are not their opinions. You must let your opinions and advice go. Simply witness. Draw up your faith they will journey the necessary road, and serve them in quiet ways.

And if they should ask your advice, before answering, remind them only *they* have the unique answer that is right for them. Offer your advice, but be brief and reinforce the truth—that this answer was right for you, at another time, in different circumstances.

that moment. It doesn't matter. Breathe. In order to be present for Janet, I became present to the anxiety inside of me and, ultimately, used my breath to calm the anxiety, focus myself, and be present. Anyone can do this. We all have access to our breath.

WE ARE STRONGER THAN WE KNOW

Even though each person's path of grief is unique, and may be difficult to witness, we can be there through it all. If we are brave enough to become still in the midst of the chaos, each moment offers its guidance. If we pay attention, we will know what to do. And little by little, as we journey into this unknown territory, the gifts will unfold. As our loved one gains a trustworthy companion, we experience an incredible depth of relationship with them. We can glimpse into our shared humanity, balance any arrogance we might have with humility, and deepen our knowledge and understanding of the seasons of the heart—a knowing that winter will turn to spring as surely as summer turns to autumn.

If you have not come to terms with the inevitable rhythms of life, you might believe you will fall apart and die in the presence of another's pain, but you won't. You might fear you don't know how to be a quiet witness, but you do. When you feel this way, it is easy to conclude that walking with grief is something you cannot do. But you can. Feeling this way is the first step toward learning something you will be called on to do again and again in your lifetime.

We are stronger than we know.

BREATHE, FORGIVE, AND LET GO

There is one true thing we can be sure of: As we try to "leave the light on" in ourselves and attempt to respond to those we love with our attention and deepest presence, we will make mistakes. We'll react to something said and interrupt. We'll give advice. We'll be distracted. We'll squirm when someone cries. We'll forget that the fear we feel when someone is expressing their grief is really more about us than them. We'll move too fast to take note of what's going on inside of us. We'll say the wrong thing. We'll judge another by our standards. We'll leave when we should stay.

And that's OK. We're human. No one expects us to be perfect, especially in such a difficult circumstance as death imposes. The important thing is to catch ourselves and try again in the next moment. Forgive ourselves and remember that we're human. Perhaps apologize if we need to, then let it go.

Forgiving ourselves is one way we learn compassion. We practice on ourselves and, in time, the kindness we nurture as we forgive ourselves spreads outward like an aura and is felt by others. Forgiveness and compassion become us.

A few years ago, several of my dearest girlfriends and I, who now live in different cities from Seattle to Miami, traveled to Tucson for a weekend together. At one time we all lived in Tucson and met as a women's group once a week for several years. I missed them every day. So I could hardly wait till we finished dinner and settled into the living room for another sweet circle. I had something I needed to talk about. These women were the perfect ones to listen. They had known me for nearly twenty years, cheered me on, seen my successes, comforted me through my losses and failures. They had loved and accompanied me through all of the major events of my thirties and forties.

With the meal finished and the dishes done, the time finally came when we curled up on the couch, chairs, and floor cushions. There was a fire in the fireplace, and a few candles lit around the room. We began to speak, one at a time, while the rest of us listened. When my turn came, I began to tell them about a new situation at work, one in which I felt painfully insecure. No sooner had I gotten a few sentences out, when two of my friends laughed raucously and began assuring me that I had nothing to worry about. They both began speaking at the same time, telling me that I was competent and capable and crazy to feel the way I was feeling. The story I was telling didn't jibe with how they imagined me to be in my professional life. The pitch of their voices kept getting louder and more insistent as I struggled to find a way to stop them.

These women are quite skilled at deep listening. They knew better, but for a moment, they simply forgot. In some ways it was sweet. They saw me as stronger than I saw myself in that moment. But that day I needed my friends to listen as I worked to discover what old conditioning was being unearthed inside that was making me feel insecure. I needed someone to listen so I could say aloud what was buried inside of me. I knew I had the answer, but I needed them to help *me* get it.

This happens all the time. Last year, as I was in the midst of writing this book, I did the same thing to one of my friends in this same group. She had to remind me that I wasn't listening! We all laughed as she said, "touché." I was embarrassed, struck by the fact that after all these years, and even as I was writing about listening, I forgot. After apologizing, I had to take a breath, forgive myself, and let it go. This is just how it is. Sometimes we have to breathe, forgive, and let go a thousand times.

I took comfort and strength from those few people who neither fled from me nor tried to save me but were simply present to me. Their willingness to be present revealed their faith that I had the inner resources to make this treacherous trek—quietly bolstering my faltering faith that perhaps, in fact, I did.

—Parker Palmer, *A Hidden Wholeness*

8
Trust Them

LANCE WAS a big, ruddy-cheeked, blond boy of twelve who had a lot of energy and was moving all the time. He was only ten years old when his mother, who was eight months pregnant, died in an automobile accident. The unborn baby died as well. Lance's father withdrew in his grief and was not available much of the time. Six months later, Lance's younger brother contracted meningitis and died very quickly. A few weeks after that, his dog was hit by a car near their home and died. Over a span of eight months, Lance had lost nearly everyone he loved, including his dog.

On the night that Lance arrived, he walked into the kids' talking circle room, a light-filled space with bright red, blue, yellow, and green pillows, and stuffed animal puppets arranged in a circle. Most kids found a spot to sit within the circle, but Lance noticed a huge mound of oversized tan and brown pillows in the corner. He ran there and dove beneath them, hiding his full body from view. The rest of the group sat down. Together we decided to leave an empty spot for him in the circle, near his "hiding place."

Sitting in Circle—Creating Sacred Space

Sitting in circle feels like the most natural thing in the world. In a circle, we can see everyone who is with us. We can look into their eyes. We can hear what they have to say. We are together. The power of circle means we are not separate. We draw on an unbroken chain of togetherness for going through anything. A circle holds everything in equilibrium.

A circle can be created with as few as two people—with a friend, a partner, or even in the workplace. You can form a circle in a bedroom, a boardroom, or anything in between. Once you've learned the art of creating a circle where people are seen, heard, and trusted, you can even do circles on the phone.

We began our kids' circle by asking them to say their names, who in their lives had died, and, if they wished to tell us the story of the death, to do so. The talking stick made its way around the circle. Each child shared something or passed the stick. When it arrived at the empty place saved for Lance, his hand popped out from under the mountain of pillows that concealed him, and he grabbed the stick. Everyone waited in anticipation for what he would say. But without uttering a word, he passed the stick on to the next kid in the circle. Week after week, for three months, he repeated the same ritual. His hand always emerged from the pillows at the perfect time. He knew exactly when his turn was. It was clear he was listening, but he hadn't said a word and we wondered if we should do more. *Should we try to coax him out? Has he been through too much trauma for our support to make an impact? How much longer should we allow him to hide under the pillows?* We tried several attempts to refer him to therapy as an adjunct to his work with us, but his family was unresponsive.

WE GRAVITATE TOWARD HEALING

I remember when, in my training, Izetta Smith at the Dougy Center said to me for the first time: "Everyone has within them everything they need to heal. Given any kind of a safe and nurturing environment, we gravitate in a direction of healing." Something inside me shifted into place, as though pieces of a puzzle deep inside had found their proper place. I knew, as surely as I knew my name, this hopeful statement was true. Its promise was that if we could create a nurturing place of safety, the following momentum toward healing was natural—supported by nature. In the years to come, it became the foundation of our philosophy at Children to Children and, after seeing it work again and again, it eventually became a central point in my worldview. I find this to be one of the up-sides of our human condition.

However, when I called Izetta with the details of Lance's story and how he was behaving in our support group, I was calling to ask, "Might *this* child be an exception?" Izetta laughed, "Marianna, Lance is just like all the others. I know his circumstances sound desperate, but in time you will see him heal—even him."

We were challenged to remember that Lance had within him everything he needed to heal from his losses. We kept re-minding ourselves, if we remained patient and gave him our faith and attention, he would heal.

Finally, one evening, Lance took the talking stick and didn't pass it on. Everyone, even the children, waited in si-lence to hear what he would say. He squirmed beneath the pil-lows and suddenly, out of the silence, we heard what sounded like a fart. It seems Lance had learned to make a farting sound with one hand squeezed under his opposite armpit—a very ap-propriate skill to learn at twelve! When we realized what he was doing, the kids rolled in laughter, and the adults—unable to contain ourselves—joined them. The room broke into pan-demonium. For several weeks afterward, Lance entertained the group into disarray by taking the talking stick and fart-ing. Each time, it took a while to regain everyone's focused attention, but because Lance was keeping the stick, we decid-ed to wait it out and not stop him from "sharing."

Then one evening when the talking stick came to him, Lance emerged from beneath the pillows with a stuffed alliga-tor puppet as his companion. He found his way into the circle and joined the rest of the children. Tentative and barely au-dible, his hand mouthed these words from within the alliga-tor's snout, "I miss my mom." He sat perfectly still for a few seconds. Then he lifted his head and passed the talking stick to the young girl sitting next to him. We all exhaled, both literally and figuratively. Later in the evening, he drew a picture of his mother.

I believe Lance had been doing deep inner work since the day he arrived. It just wasn't visible to us. His work was quiet and private, requiring several months of faith and patience on our part. It was hard to know if anything was happening within him. However, when he finally spoke, he went directly to the heart of his grief: his mom. It was a turning point for him and for us as well. After that night, he returned to the pillows on occasion, but never stayed there for long. He participated weekly with Children to Children for nearly two years.

BRIGHT FAITH, VERIFIED FAITH

Buddhists make a distinction between two different kinds of faith. One they call bright faith; the other, verified faith. When Izetta told me that within each person is everything they need, I had faith—bright faith—in that statement. I felt the truth of it and had a great respect for her wisdom; however, I had never examined it objectively for myself. My faith was untested. It rested completely on my own gut feeling, my belief in her wisdom. Probably, on some level, it felt true because I was healing.

Buddhist teachers encourage their students to examine the tenets of Buddhism for themselves. Only then does their bright faith have a chance to mature into verified faith. After my experience with Lance, I began to develop verified faith in the idea that he had within him everything he needed to heal, and the same was true for all of us. Our work had been to create a safe and loving container for him to touch on the feelings that were tender and scary. Our work had involved patience, listening, trust, and waiting. Our work had involved stopping ourselves from encouraging him to speed up his process, stopping ourselves from giving him advice, stopping ourselves from insisting he conform to our circle when it was clear he had other plans. Our work was as much an *unlearning* as it was a learning.

Lance wasn't the only child who helped us verify the truth of Izetta's claim. Many children and adults were healing just by having the time and space to move at their own pace, by having caring people around who were there to bear witness, by having the freedom to express their grief in whatever form it took, by feeling a sense of trust and acceptance in who they were during their dark time and in where they were going, whether it looked ordered or chaotic.

Kicking Away the Pain

Robert never knew his father and was ten years old when his mother died. His grandmother, whom he loved and was close to, brought him across the country to live with her and her new husband. Consequently, within a few weeks, Robert lost his home, school, neighborhood, friends, and teachers. He was an active boy who expressed his emotional turmoil through his body. Sitting still in a talking circle was difficult for him. His body was jittery, yet he bravely sat as still as he could and listened as each kid told their story. When the talking circle was done, he dashed for the Volcano Room where he would pound and bang and laugh till he fell from exhaustion. In time, he completed his work at Children to Children and the family went on with their lives.

One day Robert's grandmother, Donna, called to share a story that occurred on the anniversary of her daughter's death. Robert came home from school and asked her for a large cardboard box. She could see he'd had a tough day and something was going on, but he seemed to know what he wanted, and so she asked no questions. On the phone with me, she said she trusted that he knew, very well, how to take care of himself. Together they found a box in the garage and he took it into the backyard. As Donna watched through the kitchen window, she saw him kicking it from one end of the yard to the other and heard him grunting as he did it. "When he was done, it looked like shredded paper. You would never have known it was once a box. When he came in, he was sweaty and out of breath, but I could see he felt so much better. It was over, for now anyway."

This story struck me as a perfect example of trust. Robert was free to follow his inclinations, and Donna trusted that he knew just what he needed to take care of himself and to heal his broken heart, at least for that day. I was also delighted to see Robert had been incredibly creative. We had never done any activities at Children to Children that involved kicking boxes. At Children to Children, Robert had learned anger is a normal emotion, but not good to keep inside, and he figured out a way to release it that hurt nothing and harmed no one.

Creating the conditions for someone we love to heal from their grief can be done by anyone. It does not take a master's degree in psychology or religion, sociology, or education. Rather, it takes an open heart and the courage to resist our instinct to rescue those we love. It takes the persistent willingness to learn to listen. It asks us to let go of our judgments and preconceived notions of how our loved one "should" be grieving. It invites us into a relationship with faith—faith that everyone has within them the capacity to heal; faith in the knowledge this ability cannot be stopped, given a safe and nurturing environment. Lastly, it takes a spirit of curiosity which allows us to become a student to the person who is grieving, allowing *them to teach* us about the journey and inviting us into a place of humble witnessing.

Destructive Worry

Often when we love someone or care for them, we worry about them. But in the same way our faith in their strength and resilience can give them confidence, our worry can undermine it. It communicates a message of care contaminated by a nagging concern that they are incapable. The unintended underlying message says, "I worry about you because there is danger and it is unlikely you can handle that danger on your own."

Our common work then is 1) to notice when we are worrying about someone; 2) to breathe slowly to calm our anxious heart; 3) to separate a valid concern for their safety from an unhealthy worry that undermines their resilience; and 4) to look honestly within ourselves at our motives and patterns and begin to change our propensity for worry.

There's a common misunderstanding among all the human beings who have ever been born on the earth that the best way to live is to try to avoid pain and just try to get comfortable. You can see this even in insects, animals, and birds. All of us are the same.

A much more interesting, kind, adventurous, and joyful approach to life is to begin to develop our curiosity, not caring whether the object of our inquisitiveness is bitter or sweet.

—Pema Chödrön, *The Wisdom of No Escape*

9
A Clear Mirror

PARKER PALMER, in his book *Let Your Life Speak,* tells how a friend provided support during his own deep depression: "Blessedly, there were several people, family and friends, who had the courage to stand with me in a simple and healing way. One of them was a friend named Bill who, having asked my permission to do so, stopped by my home every afternoon, sat me down in a chair, knelt in front of me, removed my shoes and socks, and for half an hour simply massaged my feet. He found the one place in my body where I could still experience feeling—and feel somewhat reconnected with the human race.

"Bill rarely spoke a word. When he did, he never gave advice but simply mirrored my condition. He would say, 'I can sense your struggle today' or 'It feels like you are getting stronger.' I could not always respond, but his words were deeply helpful; they reassured me that I could still be seen by someone, which is life-giving knowledge in the midst of an experience that makes one feel annihilated and invisible."

Parker's friend Bill understood the principles in SALT. He slowed down and *saw* Parker just as he was, a man in the midst of a deep depression. He *allowed* Parker to be in his sorrow as long as he needed to. Bill did not try to fill the space between them with a lot of talking, but rather he *listened*—if only to their common breathing. And he *trusted* Parker would find his way out, knowing this was part of his journey to wholeness.

Their Pain Stirs Ours

In a time of loss, when someone we care about is grieving, we are shaken as well. The drama of it "catches us." We feel anxious. Our own past losses or fears about the future begin to stir. We want to take *our* pain away. So we try to take *their* pain away. Most of the time, we can't see this intermingling of emotions. We simply want to help them feel better, which is understandable. But in truth, it isn't helpful. Of course, in the end of a healing interaction, the one we love does often feel better, but we must enter the dialogue with no agenda other than to let them go where they need to go.

Sometimes the grieving person is not doing what we think they should. Maybe we think they need to get out more often, or get back to work, or create a routine, or get out of bed earlier. We want to give them advice or do *something* to put them on the "right" track. All of those things might be helpful, but the impetus for these changes will happen from within the grieving person when deeper needs are satisfied. Our job is to be still, to listen, to accept them, and love them. In that environment, they are free to move and grow at their own pace, in their own direction.

Slowing down and listening for what is truly needed is difficult and unfamiliar. *Where do we turn to learn this? How can we separate their loss from our own? What can we do to stop the*

*adrenaline rush that over-engages us in the drama of this recent
death and feeds our fear? How can we stop ourselves from talking too
much, trying to rescue, and giving advice?*

BODHICHITTA, THE AWAKENED HEART

In Buddhism, there is a Sanskrit word *Bodhichitta*. *Bodhi*
means the Awakened or Enlightened one. *Chitta* means heart,
and it also means mind. HeartMind. So, *Bodhichitta* is Awakened
Heart or Enlightened Mind. It is a wish for all of us to experience a happiness that remains with us through all the vicis-
situdes of life.

Happiness is an unusual word to introduce in a book about
our response to death, but you can trust I will not try to con-
vince you to respond to your anxiety by pretending to be happy. Rather I will explore a few ideas from Buddhism that have
helped me to relax and breathe as I face the hardships of this
life, relax and breathe as I open myself to experiencing
Bodhichitta.

One of the primary concepts the Buddha taught is impermanence, which suggests *everything* is always changing—the
weather, our bodies, our moods, birth, life, death, the tide, the
planets, the seasons. Everything is always in a state of flux.
The core nature of energy is that it moves. Everything, including us, is made of energy.

For me, having learned about death in a visceral manner
through Susan's murder, the reality of impermanence was
sewn into my consciousness before my body reached adoles-
cence. That doesn't mean I am usually comfortable with
change—far from it. But I understand the fact of impermanence from someplace deep within me. This may be one of the
gifts that came from having experienced a loss of this magni-
tude at such an early age.

Despite my understanding of impermanence, the obstacle I face, and all humans face, is the desire for predictable security and comfort. It is somehow wired into us. We like things to be the way we have known them, the way we have grown accustomed to them. Our habits and rituals are comforting. *We are hard-wired for permanence while living in an impermanent world.*

Death is the ultimate unpredictable force. We do not know how or when it will happen. Also we don't know what occurs after we die. So it is natural to experience anxiety when we're faced with death or when we're in the company of someone who is facing it.

THE WAY THINGS ARE

In order to learn how to become relaxed with uncertainty and accepting of the way things are, begin practicing with small things. Becoming comfortable with small uncertainties prepares us to become comfortable with the larger ones.

This is how it works: Try noticing the small changes of life through the lens of impermanence, changes that don't matter much—just notice them and breathe. Name them aloud if it helps. "It's beginning to rain. The weather is changing." Take a deep breath. Or "Roger has a cold and won't be at work today. Things will be different there." Breathe. Pick things that are easy to accept and just practice noticing them. "There is dust on the end table. Things don't stay clean. They change." At first this may seem silly or inconsequential—especially contrasted against the immensity of death. But we are planting a seed, and the seed has no resemblance to the orchid it will become.

Little by little we graduate to noticing more through the same lens. "Angie just had a baby. Things at home are going to be different now." Inhale slowly and exhale slowly. "I have a new manager at work. I wonder how things are going to change. I know they will." Breathe. Or "Julie's mother just died. Life is not a permanent thing." Take a deep breath. With each awareness we are acknowledging that everything changes. We have a choice: We can bemoan and resist the change. Or we can accept it—practicing and increasing our ability to relax with the unpredictability of life.

This is a lifelong practice of noticing *the way things are*. It is one way *we leave the light on*. We leave the light on so we can see everything in the room—the joy, the sorrow, the elation, the pain, the laughter, the tears, the encouragement, the scream, the smile, the living, and the dying—from a more relaxed place. We cannot control life or death. If we want to enhance the quality of life as we mature, then our daily practice is to experience change with more ease. And as we do, we increasingly release ourselves from a self-imposed prison we don't even realize we're in. We unlock the door and move freely. This freedom, coupled with compassion, will ultimately make us trustworthy companions for our grieving loved ones and everyone else in our daily life, including ourselves.

You Are Needed Right Here, Right Now

I remember, as I'm sure you do, September 11, 2001—watching the television, with horror, as airplanes flew into the World Trade Center towers. I was in San Francisco. You were in Chicago, or Toledo, or Los Angeles, or wherever. We all watched it, and we cried for every wife, husband, lover, friend, mother, father, grandparent, and child who had someone they love die there.

And then, feeling shaky but still watching our televisions on the very next day, we saw thousands of people come forward and ask, "How can I help?"

How can I help? We cried all over again, but for very different reasons. The compassion we felt and the vulnerability we experienced all translated into a desire in the hearts of so many people to offer something, anything, to others in need. People who had never been to New York got on planes and buses, drove their cars, and hitchhiked to ground zero. People volunteered their time and offered their skills wherever they were needed. In those tender days following September 11, we were all so much a part of the human race, in the very best sense.

And I thought: This outpouring of support is a beautiful thing. It's stunning, actually.

But at the same time, I wanted to get on television and say to the three hundred million people who stayed home, "You are also needed right here, right now, in your own neighborhood. Everyone you know and many others you have yet to meet are feeling a wild array of emotions. They need someone who sees them—someone who can listen generously as they regain their footing. All you need to do is pay attention all around you—in the very next moment, the very next conversation. It could be in line at the grocery store, or while putting your children to bed, or with the person who sits at the desk next to you. It will happen in the quietest moments when you least expect it. Someone will say just a few words that, if you have the ability to sense what is not being spoken—the words beneath the words—you will stop and listen so they feel the luxury and safety to say more; you will be still and offer what you can: your presence."

In grief we face a sacred moment, one permeated with fear, overflowing with pain, steeped in difficulty...the sacredness is in the sound of our returning footsteps

—Molly Fumia, *Honor Thy Children*

IO
Hard Things That Open
the Heart

I N OUR time at Children to Children, several hundred of us learned the art of being there for someone in grief by working with people we didn't know. It was our "boot camp" for learning to trust in the inherent wisdom of each human being to know what they need to do to heal. When our time at Children to Children was done, we knew how to be still and silent in the presence of the deepest grief and we brought those skills with us and used them to strengthen our relationships with the people we love—our children, our spouses, our parents, our friends. We learned that being there for another person—especially someone we love—in a time of grief brings us gifts far greater than the ones we give.

In this chapter, I share with you two stories of volunteers whose offering of deep presence transformed their families, and one story about a volunteer whose career became much more meaningful because of her newfound skills.

being there: hard things that open the heart

The Most Important Thing I've Ever Done

Laura Cohen volunteered for six years in the children's group at Children to Children. During the day she worked at a major Tucson hospital as a physical therapist. Laura's mother, Joan, was diagnosed with stage III ovarian cancer. When the doctors said Joan had only a few days to live, Laura took time off to be with her. As it turned out, Joan lived for another nine weeks, and Laura took a leave of absence to sit by her mother's side. Laura's father and brother objected to her decision, fearing she would jeopardize her career. Against the opinions and fears of the strong men in her family, Laura chose to stay with her mom, despite the risks. She wanted to have as memorable "a closing" as her own birth and childhood had been "an opening." In their extended days together, Laura physically cared for her mother as Joan's health diminished, and they had many meaningful conversations about their life together.

In Laura's words:

I never doubted that this was the right thing for me to do. It was the most important thing I have ever done in my life. Suddenly it became very clear to me how my work with Children to Children had prepared me for this time.

The principles such as: Everyone has within them the unique ability to heal themselves; grief takes as long as it takes and looks different for every person; the best gift you can give is the gift of presence, walking together, and witnessing the feelings, talking about the feelings, honoring the feelings. These life lessons profoundly impacted my personal journey and that of my family. We were blessed to have the opportunity and time to laugh, cry, and reminisce together. We spent hours telling stories, looking at pictures, napping, and just talking. My experience with other families in grief taught me to be honest, true, and present with my grief. And when the time came, I was able to help my family say goodbye. My mother was able to move on with no regrets.

When she was in hospice, and we were saying our goodbyes, my mom promised to be our "chubby little angel" looking over us. The year following my mother's death, I was offered an opportunity that involved moving across country to Pittsburgh to pursue a job and a PhD in Rehabilitation Science and Technology. In 2003, on the day I was to defend my PhD, I woke up early and it was still dark outside; there was a full moon. I had a small stained-glass angel hanging in the window, a gift from a friend of my mother's. That morning, when I closed the door to my room the reflection of the full moon cast a huge "chubby angel" on the back of the door. That had never happened before, nor since. Later that day I successfully defended my PhD. I think I'll always feel her with me.

I Knew My Feelings Were Perfectly Natural

Edward McCain, another longtime volunteer at Children to Children, stayed beyond his one-year commitment. This was a boon for us because Edward was great with the kids, and also because there always seemed to be a shortage of male volunteers. This was especially problematic because many of the children in our program had lost a father. Edward played with them, listened to them, and accompanied them on their journey to the other side of grief.

Edward's mother, Rose, with whom he was very close, moved to Tucson in her retirement to be near her son. Edward's father had died twenty years earlier, and he had no siblings—

it was just Rose and Edward. After she was diagnosed with cancer, Edward accompanied his mother to doctor appointments and was more available to help her with things she needed. Edward said, "After three years, when it became clear that the cancer wasn't going to recede, I became overwhelmed with grief and really leaned on friends and colleagues to help me. Some days, work was impossible; I struggled to process information. The reaction from others was mixed, but most people didn't know what to do with me. Thank God I had watched all those kids grieve so honestly. It gave me a lot of freedom. I knew my feelings were perfectly natural and I didn't worry about what others thought of me."

When Rose's cancer progressed to the stage where she needed more care, Edward brought her into his home to tend to her. A self-employed photographer, he also ran his business there so, near the end, they were together day and night.

"It was very challenging to be powerless in the face of cancer, a disease that inflicted so much pain on this person I loved. It made me angry that she had to suffer," he said. But during this time Edward consciously said the things he wanted her to know, and listened to the things she wanted to say. He wrote her a letter once telling her all the things he loved about her. She saved that letter. As her time of death drew near, she asked that it be read at her memorial service.

"I felt badly that, twenty years earlier when my father died, I was not there for her the way I could have been. I was still in the midst of post-adolescent rebellion and had a lot of difficulty with things that transpired between me and my father. So I wasn't there for him or her. Part of my amends that I could make for that absence was to be present for her at the end of her life. It's probably one of the things I'm most proud of—that I was able to hang in there through an excruciatingly difficult time."

In the last few days of her life, Rose entered hospice. Edward remained at her bedside, but at the very end she asked him to leave the room. As difficult as it was, he did it—with an incredible pain in his heart. A hospice worker told him she had seen that happen often. She suspected Rose asked Edward to leave because their bond was so close, she could not let go of life with him in the room. This is not the romantic, ideal picture we have of the last moments of life, but Edward was clear. "Her death had been a slow journey in which we said our goodbyes in many ways long before the minute she stopped breathing. Our life together was complete."

TODAY I STAYED

I remember one evening as our volunteers ate dinner and sat in "pre-group," a circle created to prepare us for our work with the children and adults who would be arriving within the hour. Ginny Phillips spoke. A longtime volunteer at Children to Children, Ginny was also a clinical nurse educator on the pediatric unit of a major Tucson hospital. "Nurses are typically taught to keep children alive, not how to deal with the survivors of death. Today I sat with a mother whose child died unexpectedly during the night. I was the last person to have verbal contact with her daughter. This morning, when her mother arrived at the hospital, I was able to sit and tell her what those moments with her daughter were like. I know how much that meant to her. I used to avoid conversations like this. I would slink in and rush out of their rooms. Today I stayed."

She went on to say this interaction with the mother was the kind of thing that brought a deeper meaning to her already satisfying work. It rounded out the clinical skills she possessed and taught to others. Her freedom to be able to face the whole truth of life, including death, helped her to feel complete, authentic, and unafraid.

What Is Healing?

Hardship is part of what it means to be a human being on earth. The source of pain you get in this life might be different than mine but the fact of it doesn't change. There is pain in life. But just as there is pain, there is also, within us, a primal, spiritual wholeness big enough to contain it. Having faith that hardship does not destroy our wholeness helps us to be present as we accept death, even if that death seems premature or protracted. We're less likely to spin off into our anguish about the seeming unfairness of life or entertain dire fears about our loved ones or ourselves.

What is healing? It is peace of mind. As we heal, we grow in peacefulness with what is. Many who are diagnosed with a life-threatening illness will go to great lengths to increase their chances for survival. Some will survive their disease; others will not. Healing takes place on a deep inner level that delivers us to a sense of peace about *however things turn out*. As a friend, we create a loving vessel to safely set sail together. By being present and accepting where they—and we—are at this moment, we shine a candle of faith which helps to light the way. It is the most we can do, and all that is needed.

The Truth About Tears

There are times when I am speaking to a group about Susan's murder and my eyes will well with tears and I'll feel a heat in my throat as I'm trying to speak. After all these years and so much healing, I still have moments when I *feel* her loss in my body.

When we spend our lives working to remove the barriers between our inner life and our outer life, the subtle moments of love and loss remembered in our psyche have room for expression. This expression does not mean we have neglected our grief work. Quite the opposite: It means we have done it.

The lump in my throat and the tears in my eyes don't debilitate me. They soften me. This isn't new grief, or even unresolved grief. It's an awareness of the human condition and an expression of compassion for all living beings.

This is the most profound spiritual truth I know: that even when we're most sure that love can't conquer all, it seems to anyway. It goes down into the rat hole with us, in the guise of our friends, and there it swells and comforts.

—Anne Lamott, *Traveling Mercies*

II
The Cobra's True Colors

It was an astonishing dream:

The day is sunny. I am sitting on a cement curb. My friend Jake is standing to my right and a little behind me. Another friend, Jason, is sitting beside me to the left. In the distance, a cobra snake slowly slithers its way toward us. I comment, "Look at that snake. It's a cobra. I'm going to befriend it."

Jake says, "That's stupid. It's a deadly snake." Irritated, I snap, "Jake, I'm going to become friends with this snake. You can stay or you can leave. But I'm going to do this." He glares at me then angrily walks away, mumbling that he never could figure me out.

Jason, who must feel compelled to now assume the role of protector, says, "Marianna, I'm not so sure this is a good idea. I think we need to leave." I look at him and say with calmness and clarity, "This is going to be fine. I'm not going to leave. You can join me or not, but you can't stay and try to protect me when I don't need protection. I know what I'm doing." Staring at me for a moment, he finally acquiesces. In an amazing turn-around, he puts his reservations to rest and chooses to stay and join in with full presence.

By now, the cobra is directly in front of me. I want to show him my tenderness. I begin petting his head and back, as if he were a cat or dog. The cobra coils and hisses, then glares at me and says in a gravely voice, "I could kill you. Do you understand that? I could poison you." I look into his eyes and say, "Yes. I understand your power. I know you could kill me. But I also see in you something more than your viciousness." We stare at each other—his glare, my clarity—for a long time. I take his threat seriously and stop petting him. But, strangely, I am not afraid.

After several minutes of glaring the cobra softens. In a clear and smooth voice he says, "Yes, I could kill you, but I'd really rather not. What I really want to do is show you my true col-ors." And slowly he uncoils and raises his body up. Four arms come out and the entire underbelly of the snake, including the arms, is painted in rainbow colors that glow, as though light emanates from within. Shades of pink, yellow, red, turquoise, and green are shining and undulating, bathing us with a light show that seems to penetrate the surface of our skin, to make a way into the inside of us. We gasp at the magnificence of this vision. And the cobra remains for a very long time as we stare in awe, infused in luminescence and color.

This is exactly how it is when we are deeply present and really see someone. When trust is developed and all agendas are dismissed, there comes a time, as in my dream, when one's true colors emerge and we simply look and see them. When this happens, everyone can feel it. There is nothing else like it in the world.

No matter what a person may present on the surface, I believe what they really want is to show their colors. They want to be seen. These moments tiptoe in with a comment like Judy's that said, "I wish my mom were here." Or like Lance, they use humor to mask a hurt, or hiss their anger in order to protect themselves. This is not to say all humor or anger is a cover-up for something else. Rather, there is often a larger story beneath the one we initially hear. This understanding of human nature is a call to be still and listen, be still and watch, be still and see. To do this, we slow down and adjust our eyes to the "pace of seeing." It may take us a lifetime to learn this. But the older I get, the more I realize most of the important things I have learned have taken a long time. This is why we "leave the light on" day after day and remain awake to the experiences life presents us.

Sometimes it means turning off *our* need to be seen for a short while, or suppressing our fear and its accompanying need to protect and give advice. Other times it means stopping the act of judging someone and, instead, becoming a student learning about this person. These efforts are worth a lifetime of attention and practice. As far as I can tell, they are the only way we become privileged to bear witness to another's true colors.

~~~

In her book *Traveling Mercies: Some Thoughts on Faith*, author Anne Lamott writes: "All those years I fell for the great palace lie that grief should be gotten over as quickly as possible and as privately. But what I've discovered since is that the lifelong fear of grief keeps us in a barren, isolated place and that only grieving can heal grief; the passage of time will lessen the acuteness, but time alone, without the direct experience of grief, will not heal it.... We are a world in grief, and it is at once intolerable and a great opportunity. I'm pretty sure that it is only by experiencing that ocean of sadness in a naked and immediate way that we come to be healed—which is to say, that we come to experience life with a real sense of presence and spaciousness and peace."

Many people don't allow themselves to go to that "barren, isolated place" after someone they love has died. Understandably so. If they do, it is often with much reluctance and mostly privately. But if there is someone in the grieving person's life who can be trusted, someone who is relaxed in the presence of sorrow, anger, or depression, someone who has no agenda or advice to give, someone who has faith their grieving companion will survive and one day thrive—then isolation does not have to be the grieving person's only choice.

See them. Allow them. Listen to them. Trust them. Let the SALT of their tears teach us how to love them well in this time of inconsolability. Let it remind us that each person must feel their own feelings in their own order, their own time, not by our clock or our standards. Allow it to *show* us what the Buddha meant when he said life has ten thousand joys *and* ten thousand sorrows.

Let us be the candle of faith for the person we love when their own flame is flickering low. May this love inspire courage in our heart as we stretch into new territory. Let our burgeoning trust in their ability to heal inspire patience because now we know this sojourn can take many turns and also a very long time. May we bear witness and breathe into our own trembling heart as it grows and strengthens.

Let us adopt a spirit of curiosity so that our arrogance—the part of us that thinks it knows more than it actually does—can dissolve. This is when humility finds a welcome home inside us, and light pours in as though a wall has been removed. This is when our bright faith blossoms into verified faith to deliver *a knowing* that assures us the one we love has within them everything they need, with the exception of a friend to bear witness; *a knowing* we have the capacity to be that friend and to embrace their suffering, if they so choose; *a knowing* that ushers in a deeper, more satisfying experience of life as it truly is.

IN THE OTHER KIND OF TIME

Let's journey now
to the other kind of time
where we've known each other
for centuries, beneath our names,
beneath our pain, to the other side
where we can stop to listen
the way fox listen to the night.

Come with me out of the cold
where we can put down the
notions we've been carrying
like torn flags into battle.

We can throw them to the earth
or place them in the earth, and ask,
why these patterns in the first place?
If you want, we can repair them, if
they still seem true. Or we can
sing as they burn.

Come. Let's feel our way
beneath the noise where we
can ask what it means to be alive
and lift our chins from the stream
like deer who've outrun
all the hunters.

—Mark Nepo

Afterword
Being and Doing

Most of what's included in *Being There for Someone in Grief* is about how to **be** with someone who is grieving—what's required of us to be deeply present to the whole blessing and catastrophe of life and death. Yet you may find yourself asking the question, "But there must be something I can **do** to help."

There are some very simple, basic guidelines for what to **do** that naturally emerge with experience if we are sensitive to the vulnerability of loss. This chapter will give you a few guidelines for what you can offer to do in this challenging time.

Most of the time the person who is grieving cannot tell us what they need, so I have written this chapter in their voice. If they could be articulate, clear headed, and thoroughly comfortable asking for help, this is what they might say. And remember: Listen more than you speak and let go of any idea of how you want it to be.

Being and Doing

- *Beauty is soothing. Bring fresh flowers when you visit. Offer to take me somewhere in nature for a walk. Send me a beautiful card. Give me a photo you might have of the person who died. Bring me a candle. Light it. Straighten up my home (if you are a close friend and I have given you permission). Sweep my front porch. Water the flowers there. Mow my lawn. Plant a tree in honor of the person who died and take me there to see it.*

- *Tell me what you remember about the person who died. Write me a story about him. Tell me a story about a time she and I were together that you remember.*

- *I may be feeling scattered. Offer to help with details of the funeral; pay my bills; pick up my children; call friends to tell them the news; drive me somewhere; wash the car; do my grocery shopping; call my place of employment to tell them I won't be at work. Purchase a guest book for the memorial service.*

- *I may have no appetite. Remind me to eat, but don't insist. If I say yes, prepare a meal. Get me out of the house by taking me out for a meal. Bring food in so that I don't have to leave the house. Ask me about food preferences or allergies.*

- *I may forget about my body and its needs. Remind me to drink water. Bring me a glass of water. Suggest that we take a walk. Schedule a massage (ask me first). Give me a foot rub. Make a hair or manicure appointment for me. Take me there. Leave apples and pears on my front porch.*

- *After the memorial service, leave a phone message to tell me you're thinking of me. Keep this up long after everyone else has resumed their lives and I am alone. If I am sending out thank you notes, buy stamps for me. Offer to handwrite the addresses; ask first and be OK if I say no. It's not about you. Take me to the movies.*

- *When you're with me, don't fill all the space with words. Let the pace and content of our conversations be led by me. Don't turn away if tears bubble up—in me or in you. Say "I'm sorry that you're hurting," then be quiet. You don't need to have all the answers. Sometimes just being there—and being a loving presence—is enough.*

Generosity—our ability to offer the best of who we are and what we have for the benefit of one another—is perhaps our most valuable human attribute. In fact, it may be the singular quality we possess that has the capacity to transform the world.

—Wayne Muller

Pay It Forward

Being There for Someone in Grief is filled with stories of healing—stories made possible because of many generous people who kindly came forward to help, to give of themselves in order to *be there* for someone in their darkest hour. These simple acts of generosity are priceless because they restore our faith in humanity. They inspire us to be more generous because, in our hearts, *this is the kind of world we want to live in, the kind of world we want to leave as our legacy.* Creating a culture of care begins personally, with me and with you. *We* are the ones we've been waiting for.

Our own personal healing is inextricably linked to the healing of others. Each of us is connected to those who suffer —no matter the circumstances of their pain, or ours. Our liberation is made possible by attending to their healing.

If you have been nourished in some way by what you have read, please pass it on. I offer two suggestions on the following pages. Because the more we realize what we have been given, and feel the unmistakable warmth of gratitude in our heart, the more it inspires us to give something to someone else, and keep the gift flowing.

Pay It Forward
The Susan Brady Fund

One evening in our talking circle at Children to Children a young boy said, "Before I came here, on a scale of one to ten, I was a zero. Now I'm a six." We asked him how a six acts differently than a zero and he said, "Well, before, when I used to get angry, I would pound on other kids. Now I scream into my pillow or hit my bed. I don't beat up other kids anymore."

Some of the children we served were angry and living in environments where violence had been acted out. We told them anger was a common feeling but one that wasn't OK to express by hurting ourselves or another. We showed them various things they could do to move the energy out of their bodies. Any one of the children could have possibly grown up without any healthy interventions, leaving them with a pain so big they might kill another. History will never record the tragedies prevented here.

I opened a fund to benefit the Children to Children program at Tu Nidito in honor of Susan Brady. If you would like to help it flourish, you can mail a gift of any amount to:

Tu Nidito *"Your Little Nest,"* 3922 N. Mountain Ave., Tucson, AZ 85719-1313.

Please note in the memo: *The Susan Brady Fund.*

PAY IT FORWARD
THE BEING THERE FUND

Once, in a conversation with a prison chaplain, he told me in his lifetime of working with those who are incarcerated, he had yet to come across someone who had not suffered a terrible loss—most happened when the incarcerated person was young.

A fund has been created at Bread for the Journey for gifting this book to those who could benefit from its teachings, and would not have access. They will be made available—free of charge—to people in prisons and juvenile detention centers; donated to places where tragedy has occurred; placed in hospital libraries, hospice settings and at grief support centers, etc.

If you have been touched by the teachings in this book and wish to pay it forward, direct your donation to Bread for the Journey's "Being There Fund."

Mail to Bread for the Journey: 267 Miller Ave., Mill Valley, CA 94941.

Please write "Being There Fund" in the memo.

You may also donate online at: www.breadforthe journey.org. Click the DONATE button on the homepage, and select "Being There Fund."

Photo: Greg McGlaze

About the Author

Marianna Cacciatore is an author and grief support consultant living in the San Francisco Bay Area. She works privately—by phone and in person—to support people in grief, and those who want to *be there* for them. She speaks to audiences worldwide, and consults with organizations regarding grief support programs. (www.mariannacacciatore.com)

She serves as a Lifetime Emeritus Board Member of Tu Nidito *"Your Little Nest,"* the parent agency for Children to Children. (www.tunidito.org)

Marianna serves as Executive Director of Bread for the Journey, a national philanthropic organization dedicated to nurturing the seed of generosity in every human heart. (www.breadforthejourney.org)

When relaxing, she mostly plays with her sweetheart, Greg, and their dog, Gia, at their home in Marin County, California.

Grief Support

For grief support services in your city, go to The Dougy Center's website at dougy.org and select GRIEF SUPPORT RESOURCES. To work with this author, go to marianna cacciatore.com and select CONTACT.

LaVergne, TN USA
21 April 2010
179983LV00003B/1/P